RUNNIN' WITH THE BIG DOGS

RUNNIN' WITH THE BIG DOGS

The True, Unvarnished Story of the Texas-Oklahoma Football Wars

MIKE SHROPSHIRE

WM

WILLIAM MORROW
An Imprint of HarperCollinsPublishers

HarperCollins books may be purchased for educational, business, or sales promotional use. For information please write: Special Markets Department, HarperCollins Publishers, 10 East 53rd Street, New York, NY 10022.

FIRST EDITION

Designed by Renato Stanisic

Library of Congress Cataloging-in-Publication Data has been applied for.

ISBN-13: 978-0-06-085277-1
ISBN-10: 0-06-085277-1

06 07 08 09 10 NMSG/RRD 10 9 8 7 6 5 4 3 2 1

To Sadie and Curly

Contents

CONTENTS

Author's Note

Grown Men Behaving Badly

S ome of this story is written from the first-person perspective. That's for a couple of reasons. First, it's obviously easier to tell any story from that point of view if you can. And second, I have been close enough to the core of the topic and have ventured to the periphery of the arena, and I know what it sounds like down there, to tell it that way. Obviously, there's a cast of god-knows-how-many-thousand other people who've ventured more deeply into the cauldron than me. Which is why I'm not in here much, just around long enough to set the scene a few times.

Oklahoma and Texas played for the one hundredth time in October 2005. My first awareness of the festivities happened fifty-five years ago.

My father, just like Sam Houston and Davy Crockett, had once been involved in Tennessee politics and had come to Texas, in part, because maybe things were not all that great back home. Daddy never went off to live with the Indians, the way Houston did, but according to his 2003 obituary, he had been "rescued by the aborigine off the coast of New Guinea when his B-25 was shot down in 1943." For a long time, my wife suspected all of that was bullshit. Then one night I heard her say, "Spencer, is it true that in World War II, a bunch of pygmies saved your life?"

"No," he said, then paused before adding in that amazing voice of his that sounded as if it had been aged in those oaken casks in Lynchburg where they produce the bourbon he consumed so prodigiously throughout his years. "Not pygmies, necessarily. But very peculiar little people."

Therefore, in light of that, when my old man would later describe a particular Texas-OU football weekend—the one in 1950—as "the damndest thing I ever saw," it must have been a doozy. He had two old pals from back in Tennessee—one of 'em was a major general in the Tennessee Air National Guard—who flew around the country in some old bomber, taking care of whatever state business that needed tending at the sites of major college football games and heavyweight championship fights. In 1950, they flew to Dallas.

Why not? Oklahoma was number one in the nation. Texas was number two. So they checked into the Adolphus hotel in downtown Dallas—the Plaza of the plains, the Waldorf-Astoria of the white-trash nation. My father would join them there, and during the Friday afternoon pregame, one of his old Tennessee cronies (let's call him Snead, totally unrelated to a UT quarterback with the same name) stumbled across a scene at the front desk. A chauffeur-driven rich lady from one of America's northern provinces upon registering at the hotel expressed alarm at the uncivilized decorum of the football celebrants in the lobby, a bacchanalian assembly of two-fisted jug boxers. Poor woman. She'd selected the wrong weekend to visit Dallas and shop at Neiman Marcus, which was right next door to the Adolphus. Now some Texas fan was trying to feed beer to her poodle. The desk clerk tried to calm her. There was not another room available within a hundred miles. She was stuck there with the riffraff, for a night at least. Snead heard all, then secured her room number.

At 7 A.M. on Saturday, game day, Snead called the woman's suite.

"Good morning, Mrs. Vanderslice," Snead said. "This is Walton Fairchild, manager of the Adolphus, and on behalf of the hotel, I would like to offer you our profound apology for any inconvenience caused you by some of our guests. So please, on behalf of the hotel, enjoy breakfast in the dining room with our compliments. And now . . . IT'S TIME TO GET YOUR FAT YANKEE ASS OUTTA BED!"

My father loved to tell that story, repeated it most of his life, but what stuck with me about the 1950 Texas-OU game was this other morsel he brought back from the football arena. Even an ignorant third-grade kid could identify the enormity of this number-one-versus-two concept when it entailed the entire United States. So I could imagine the magnitude of what must have been happening over in Dallas, where you could probably feel the ground shake. Oklahoma won the game, 14–13. My father was no longer convinced that football beyond the Southeast Conference didn't amount to much. "Even though Texas lost, one of the best players on the field was a guy named [Bobby] Dillon. Defense back. All-American. And he's got one eye, and I wonder if somehow Oklahoma took advantage of that."

It's the kind of thing that makes a third-grade kid want to stop and think.

Introduction

The Whiskey Feud

This is the story of an event that exploits violence and promotes extravagantly irresponsible and destructive behavior among the persons who attend it.

Thousands upon thousands of football fans from two states, their brains united into a single altered state, arrive annually at the Cotton Bowl stadium, bellowing exhortations for the spillage of blood. The Texas-Oklahoma game, which now has been conducted one hundred times, and all that surrounds it, has arisen into the manliest of spectacles and is genuinely about as politically incorrect as you can get. You'll find audiences more genteel and reserved at cockfights. This game encourages the forces of overindulgence and leaves behind an eventual trail of not only tears but shattered cocktail glasses and memories of fornication gone awry.

Why, then, produce a book that shamelessly celebrates this sociological embarrassment—this lurid tattoo that exists only to desecrate the backside of law and order?

Because the Texas-Oklahoma game, while not bigger than life, is more than a game. Here is why: the attendees of this football conflict, which happens annually in Dallas, unselfishly contribute countless hours of court-mandated community service, and many charities and faith-based organizations couldn't make it without their help. Were it not for Texas-OU weekend, AA would have to fold. So the community has become the trickle-down beneficiary of the football game, justifying its yearly reenactment, raw though it is.

When I was covering college football for various newspapers, I attended and wrote about games that were played at the home stadiums of every Division I school in Texas and the states that surround it, with the exception of New Mexico. Additionally, I covered games at Nebraska, Iowa, Wisconsin, Purdue, Ohio State, Penn State, Georgia Tech, Auburn, Tennessee, Miami, Arizona State, Washington, West Point, Stanford, and Cal. Those credentials remain insufficient for qualification as an expert witness, but I do consider myself reasonably exposed to the blue-sky autumn festival of the sport at some of its most enduring five-star settings.

At this point, I am supposed to say that, compared to Texas-OU, these other presentations are string-quartet parlor-music affairs. That isn't the case. When it comes to big-time college football, there aren't any bad concerts. Yet this Texas-OU thing leaves you deaf.

I was in the stands for one of the storied rivalry games, Michigan-Ohio State, the 1977 game at Ann Arbor, and still I like Texas-OU better. That is largely due to the fact that at Ann Arbor, I didn't care which team won, and, because it was nine degrees above zero, it was hard to see the action on the field through everybody's steaming breath. That's one game that could benefit from a neutral site for sure. Ohio State–Michigan at Wrigley Field, every Halloween night. Now, that would be a show.

This neutral-site format really does jazz the excitement quotient, too. There are only a couple of others, and I'm pretty sure Texas-OU beats them. Florida and Georgia play their game in

Jacksonville. I have a daughter who lives there, and she says the only nightlife consists of getting drunk at Chili's. And then, of course, there's Army-Navy. Somehow, and maybe I'm wrong, it's hard for me to fathom the notion of the proud alums of Annapolis and West Point running naked through the corridors of the best hotels in Philadelphia and throwing lamps out of the windows.

That's the charm of the October Oddness in Dallas. Now the great gathering is being threatened by a few popinjays, peckerwoods, and pencil-neck geeks who want to take the thing out of Dallas for reasons that they say involve finance. Some people operating within the sanctimoniously coated realm of university officialdom think that a home-and-home rendering of the Texas-Oklahoma game would be more practical since the Cotton Bowl stadium in Dallas—the very womb of football heritage—has gotten kinda old and saggy and nobody loves her anymore. Critics complain about a lack of concession stands, and women have spoken of the inconvenience of standing in line for about six years to take a leak. While Fair Park, comfortable, with art deco charm, is a terrific spot for a football stadium and a classic game like Texas-OU, the surrounding neighborhoods resemble the scene of an airline disaster. The Big D economic development people like to tout the area's two booming growth industries: breaking and entering. You can't find slums this sinister in Manila.

The city of Dallas is pondering a renovation of the stadium to increase the seating in hopes that the teams will stick around. In May 2006, UT belatedly agreed to continue the Dallas event through 2010. Beyond that, politics will determine that Texas-OU and the Cotton Bowl will part company forever. Some say the competition will maintain its breathtaking vigor. Some say that the Mardi Gras would be better if they staged *it* home-and-home in Beaumont and Hattiesburg because that's where all the partyers come from in the first place. While they're at it, let's run the Kentucky Derby in Toledo and Dearborn, in rotating years, since Churchill Downs is such a dump.

Whatever happens, my plan to beat the system is shot for good. The centerpiece of the State Fair of Texas is, naturally, a Ferris wheel that people can see from miles away. Biggest Ferris wheel in North America, and when you ride the thing and it stops at the absolute top, you see the vistas of the Dallas skyline glistening in the late afternoon sun and the kaleidoscopic swirl of the fairgrounds below. Most people stand in the long line and finally get on, but when it sits up top, they don't like it worth a damn. They're scared to look straight down. But if they did, here's what else they could see—a little bit more than half of the playing field in the Cotton Bowl, from the tip of the goalpost in the south end zone out just past the fifty.

My scheme had been to bribe the Ferris wheel operator with a couple of cartons of Camels and have him stop the thing with my little cage on top and tell everybody that the ride broke down. Meanwhile, I'd be up there swaying in this on-top-of-the-world cage and watching great football action while everybody else is being led down from the thing on those long fire-engine ladders. When they build up those end-zone stands, one more dream will be lost for good. Any narrative composed on the Texas-OU phenomenon would be incomplete without an account of the game from that Ferris wheel perspective, and this one will have to make do without it.

This is not intended as a traditional history of the one-hundred-game series, but rather just a discussion of the panorama. An issue of *Sports Illustrated* that appeared in early December 2005 contained several pages of the best work of photographer Neil Leifer, who'd recently died. The assortment included a photo of Vince Young and his coach, Mack Brown, hands on knees, on the sideline of the '05 Texas-OU game. In contrast to that was a black-and-white shot of Darrell Royal from the game in 1963—in command, kneeling on the sideline and gazing at the action on the field, backed by his crew-cut corps of earnest faces. Much of this book is devoted to that season, the one framed in black and white. I was young then, my fascination with Texas-OU was at its zenith, and I was acquainted with some of the players.

Then as now there's a certain gallantry of bearing that characterizes the people who actually played in the game. Brave, courageous, and bold, like the theme song from Wyatt Earp, these men, on the whole, were so secure in who they were, so healthy of self-concept, that they never abused children, animals, or well-behaved women. I am not naïve enough to suggest that participants in the game haven't entered the fray fortified by every performance-enhancing product known to man and nature. One could reasonably also assume that Texas-OU games have been played in which every player on the field had a substantial wager on the outcome. Naturally, I am not suggesting that anybody ever bet *against* his team, although the UT-OU wager might have been part of a three-team parlay. On the whole, though, the fellows in the State Fair scrum functioned in life, and on the field, as white-hat cowboys, devoting their lives to the chase of thieving rustlers and the rescue of distressed damsels.

How frequently now we pick up the sports section and read something about some ex-professional football player who killed himself drinking antifreeze. One Prestone and tonic too many.

That kind of ending would never befall an honorably discharged veteran of the Dallas fray. You don't read about a Texas-OU man being torn asunder by antifreeze. Might make 'em sick, but it wouldn't kill 'em.

1

You're Doing a Heckuva Job, Brownie

Either way it went, I knew it was going to hit the old-timers pretty hard, those UT guys now living on the shabby side of sixty. The anxiety that was building by the kickoff of that Rose Bowl was boiling out of the pot and hissing on the stove. The ones who didn't travel to Pasadena chose to watch the game at home, and alone. Husbands and wives mostly watched it in separate rooms. She knew what was going to happen, that he would be swinging around on the overhead light fixtures like some opium-crazed baboon, and she couldn't stand the sight of him by the fourth quarter. Southern Cal was handling the Longhorns, and, uh-oh, there went Reggie Bush, finally, and the man in the next room, he was not saying anything, but he was glaring hard at the new Samsung HDTV, and then he had an empty wine bottle in his right hand and was winding up like Roger Clemens. The only reason he didn't bring the high hard one is because he didn't have the guts to throw it. He put down the bottle and shouted at the television set. "Reggie Bush stole the Heisman, flat stole it, 'cause he went and gained a half a mile against Fresno State. Well, lemmee tell you what ol' Coach Thornton—God, was he a m-e-e-e-a-n sonufabitch—what he taught us in the eighth grade. THERE'S NO SUCH THING AS AN ALL-AMERICAN HALFBACK! THERE *IS* SUCH A THING AS CHICKENSHIT TACKLING!"

In one Austin household, the tension became so dire that an old and loyal follower of the Orange employed his Last Resort ritual, which dates back to the 1969 Arkansas game, in which he puts his wallet on the TV set and sings "The Eyes of Texas" in Spanish, knowing full well that if there's stress in the marriage already, that little show won't do it much good. Back in Dallas, a man that we'll call Brad, UT class of '76, decided to take his Fourth Quarter Rally Whiz in his front yard. So while he did, his wife locked him out. Texas women are tough, and they're mean as hell, too. One had thought about concealing a video camera in the den so she could surprise the old Horn with the tape in the morning when he'd already be hung over and sad; let the fool see himself in action and then show it to the kids and put it on the Internet. That's one of the essential reasons that the 2005 Texas team was such a joy to its fan base; it was a lovely diversion from the harder demands of domestic reality and the cruelties of the work world.

These UT alums are ferociously loyal to the school. They might not have learned very much, at least inside the classroom. Yet to a person, everyone I ever knew who went to that school in Austin had a rip-roaring good time and afterward enjoyed prosperous business careers selling stuff to one another. God, they were revved for this USC battle for the Bowl Championship Series (BCS) championship game, but they weren't blind to the task of trying to stop the Trojans' LenDale White, who would be crashing relentlessly onward behind those linemen from the Pacific Isles, the ones the size of Texaco stations.

It got tense when the fourth-and-two play, the moment of truth, High Noon, came to pass in the fourth quarter, Trojans up by six and the life draining ever so gravely from the game clock. In a Texas den, a man with wispy white hair was on the floor on all fours, pawing the oak hardwood and shouting, "Dig deep, men! Grab a root and growl!" When Vince Young crossed the goal line with nineteen seconds to play in the Rose Bowl game, senior Longhorns felt that their collective lifetime experience on planet Earth was verified as something worthwhile. When the game was finally over, they clutched their chests and fell to the floor while their wives crept cautiously into the room, inquiring, "Do you want me to call 911?"

No. Within minutes, old Longhorns throughout the land had struggled back to their feet, knowing the moment of Young running the ball on fourth down to defeat those cocky-ass Trojans—the team that nine of ten media people in Pasadena deemed unbeatable by Texas or anybody else—would be etched in their memory banks for the remainder of their days. So instead of calling an ambulance, by midnight they were on the phone to people they had not spoken with for two generations, shouting, "Can you fuckin' believe it!"

So Coach Mack Brown and the Longhorns won the national college football championship, the first time Texas had done that in thirty-five years. Lee Corso, the ex-coach and ESPN commentator, was on television the morning after in full gush, claiming that the win over USC was the greatest game, at any level, in the history of football. For fans who were old enough to recall the last time UT had won the national title, this Rose Bowl happening was like watching their thirty-five-year-old kid finally graduate from high school. After all those years of underachievement, he not only finished but would be valedictorian of the whole damn class.

Everyone gathered at the temple on Sunday night, a week later, amid a merchandising frenzy that was as hot as the drought-driven wildfires that were threatening to devour the whole state. At Darrell K. Royal–Texas Memorial Stadium, the upper decks were closed, but about 50,000 jammed into the rest of the lower grandstands to see the confirmation ceremony. Away from the stadium the famous and ever-conspicuous UT stood bathed in orange light, and lights in the windows were arranged to make a numeral 1. People could see that for miles and miles, from nearby I-35, aka the NAFTA Expressway and from the distant twinkling hilltops that look down upon Austin from the west. Sometime around 1961, an issue of a UT humor magazine called *The Texas Ranger Dispatch* came out featuring a cover illustration of the grand old tower with a condom on it.

Now they'd built a stage on the south end zone, that garden of memories where the Longhorns always seemed to make their most historic touchdowns for some reason, down on the scoreboard end. The JumboTron was showing Rose Bowl highlights. Fourth and two, and down goes LenDale White! The crowd had seen all of this somewhere before, but they cheered anyway. They cheered again and again as Young, the man of many gifts, shepherded his forces on that final drive. Vince Young is not simply a once-in-a-lifetime college quarterback. Young is more a product of some PlayStation game, like that gladiator in Mortal Kombat who disappears on you. Vince is just like that, and imagine trying to tackle somebody supernatural. One instant, he's here, and the next, he's there, in the end zone, and the defenders gape at one another, dumbfounded as to how that was accomplished. The stirring climax came almost as if scripted by the Steven Spielberg people.

With the fourth-quarter clock ticking inside thirty seconds, grinding toward the eternity that would begin at 0:00, a member of the Texas bar, his face bloated up like a dead whale, screamed, "For God's sake! File a motion for continuance!" When Young went gliding into the end zone so cool and erect and dramatically ideal for the cover of *Sports Illustrated,* there was a sliver of time left for Matt Leinert and the Trojans to ruin things yet. Each one of those last nineteen seconds seemed to pass slower than a workday in Genesis. Last summer I saw what was sort of the Rose Bowl of Irish football, County Cork versus County Clare, and a sportswriter for *The Irish Times* wrote the next day that the game was one of those occasions when lads become men and mortals become gods. What a game.

It's always a delight to maintain residency in Austin, where people are paid by the state to do nothing except be cool and laid back. Live music on every street corner. Tex-Mex, three meals a day. People wearing bathrobes to the grocery store, the same store where you'll see Sandra Bullock standing in a long line to receive a free Blue Bell ice-cream cone. They'd been talking about fitting out the UT football team in sandals with cleats. Now, on the Sunday of the national championship ceremony, many of these Austinites were so excited, they couldn't even go get a new tattoo.

Up on the stage, Governor Rick Perry showed off the pair of sealskin cowboy boots that he'd won off Governor Terminator in their Rose Bowl bet. "We beat the hell out of Southern Cal!" the governor was shouting. But was it real? Rick Perry used to be a Texas Aggie yell-leader, and if that doesn't make him a true-blue Aggie, then I don't know what does, and any true-blue Aggie hates these liberal-leanin', tea-sippin' UT bastards like Jesus hates sin. But he looked sincere.

United States Senator Kay Bailey Hutchison couldn't be accused of any such conflict of interest. The first time Texas won the football championship, in 1963, the senator was on the

UT sideline leading cheers. The cheerleaders then were not anything like the cheerleaders now, with their quadruple backflips and shameful, navel-exposing uniforms. When the senator was doing that, the cheerleaders wore skirts that came down near their ankles, and I'll bet that Kay Bailey Hutchison couldn't do a cartwheel. She was on the stage now, gloating big-time. Here was the bottle of California wine that Dianne Feinstein had delivered. That was the stake in the wager between the senators, a bottle of California wine against a bottle of Texas wine. (What was Senator Feinstein thinking? She loses either way.)

The senator presented the wine to Mack Brown. Mack didn't need any wine. He was sitting up there with the Grail. The BCS trophy. The old crystal pigskin. See how it glitters. Simply touch the prize from Pasadena and experience three-glasses-of-hundred-dollar-champagne-on-an-empty-stomach magic. Mack Brown sat there with the glass football trophy and caressed it like a kitty cat. Brown wore a face that was aglow with redemption, and his eyes shouted, "I told you so!" The man who couldn't win the big one had just won the biggest game of all time. And to think of all the horse crap this poor man has had to endure, dating back to when he and his brother Watson Brown were trying to establish winning football programs at basketball colleges and Steve Spurrier, at Florida, was calling them the Lose Brothers. Everybody liked Mack.

Brown stood up to speak, looking out at all those faces, true believers now. Not so long ago, these same happy, cheering faces were the ones popping off at the Shoal Creek Saloon, crowded on Pork Chop Tuesday, loud enough to be overheard at several nearby tables: "That Mack Brown. He sure looks great at a barbecue, standing there talking to the big shots. But get him on the sideline in a game that matters, and he could fuck up an Easter egg hunt."

Mack put all of that to rest at midseason of 2004. He and offensive coach Greg Davis ran the entire playbook through a paper shredder and came up with a whole new attack. It consisted of two plays: Vince left and Vince right, and the Longhorns hadn't lost a game since. See how easy that was? Plain as that sounds, Brown accomplished the strategic coaching ploy of college football's decade to date.

Brown had four players stand up and talk. David Thomas, senior tight end from Out in Middle of Nowhere, Texas, who caught ten balls in the Rose Bowl game. Senior tackle Rod Wright, part of the pile that LenDale White couldn't move on the fourth-down short-yardage try that turned the game. Michael Griffin, who'd made that splendid end-zone interception against USC in the second quarter, floating in the air like a Russian ballerina to pick off Matt Leinert, got up and apologized to teammate Terrell Brown for running into him and breaking his arm. An offensive lineman, Justin Blaylock, told the fans that he was not entering the NFL, even though he'd go low first round, so he could stick around and kick some asses in the Big 12 Conference.

For Vince Young, this would be his farewell performance at Memorial Stadium. His fourth-and-five journey into the archives was shown up on the JumboTron again. The people cheered and Vince waved and, knowing that he'd done all he could do for these people, he would ride on. Throughout the season, there was much discussion of how Vince Young had taught Mack Brown to have some fun in life. Hell, he was making a hundred times more money than Darrell Royal, back when Texas was winning those championships from yesterday. Young provided his coach with a music-appreciation course and indoctrinated him to a different genre of rhythm and noise, and all of a sudden Coach Brown wasn't Coach Brown anymore, he was Daddy Mack, no longer the straight-arrow Dixie who had been wound up tighter than the inside of a golf ball because he couldn't beat Oklahoma. Vince taught Daddy Mack how to chill, and while Mack Brown never skipped practice to go boogie to the tunes of Afro Freque at the Flamingo Cantina, that didn't mean that he might not someday. Mack Brown's 2005 team, with the flourish at the end of that miraculous Rose Bowl game, not only guaranteed that the Longhorns' most ardent followers would die happy but also enabled them a positive beginning in the hereafter.

A fireworks show ended the five-star Longhorns gala night. A lot of people were thanked and acknowledged. But while Brown and UT athletic director DeLoss Dodds and all the rest were passing out the gratitude, they forgot to thank the one person most responsible for putting together this show.

Bob Stoops, head coach of the Oklahoma Sooners.

Maybe Mack Brown should have given that bottle of Feinstein wine to Stoops. It was out of the fire-eating urgency to somehow beat Bob Stoops and Oklahoma that Brown collected his team and made key and expensive additions to his coaching staff. Brown knew that the only way to beat OU would be to put together the best team in the United States. Which he did. Mack Brown's 2005 lineup included a big assortment of senior players who were national 100 prep talent. Michael Huff, a secondary star, and offensive tackle Jonathan Scott were charted as NFL talent, along with defensive tackle Rod Wright, safety Cedric Griffin, and tight end David Thomas. And of course his magnificence himself, Vince Young, who had hardly materialized from the mists. Recruiting services had rated Young as the top prospect in the United States as a senior at Madison High in Houston. That's a helluva lot of talent, a terrific arsenal for a college team, and it was assembled for one reason.

That was to beat Oklahoma. Beating USC in the greatest game in the history of football was an afterthought.

That's the beauty of the Texas-Oklahoma football series, a century-old rivalry that consists not of win streaks but mood swings that are menopausal in magnitude. It has worked like this:

When the Longhorns ruled the series during the World War II years, Oklahoma hired Bud Wilkinson to figure out a way to beat those Texas bastards. The consequence of that found Wilkinson constructing the best football team in the land, the best anybody had ever seen.

Darrell Royal was summoned to put a stop, somehow, to the Oklahoma onslaught. Royal groomed teams that were so fast, aggressive, and chillingly efficient in all phases of the game that they beat Oklahoma and, as a byproduct, won three national titles. In the course of doing that, Royal beat OU twelve times in thirteen games.

What the Sooners did to break the streak in 1971 was to introduce a team under Chuck Fairbanks that was so rip-roaringly great that neither Texas nor any team in the NCAA could slow them down. Barry Switzer took the '71 scorched-turf template and built teams with awesome capabilities. On the occasions that OU did not win the national championship, it was usually because Penn State or Miami got lucky.

Enter Bob Stoops. His 2000 team marched into Dallas and beat Texas, 63–14. Afterward, Mack Brown apologized to the university, to the fans, to his players, to the great state of Texas; hell, Mack said he was sorry to everybody but the People's Republic of China. Meanwhile, Bob Stoops laughed, won the BCS title game against Florida State, and never looked back.

What would Mack Brown have to do to compete with Stoops? Ask USC.

The eternal cycle of the Texas-Oklahoma football series is one of self-regenerating greatness.

Now, even without Vince Young, Mack Brown's Longhorns

are a potent force, fabulously talented, and their new QB will probably be—are you ready for this—Colt McCoy, from Jim Ned High School in Tuscola, Texas. His name alone would be worth a touchdown and a half, even before the kickoff.

Meanwhile, Stoops and the Sooners are seething to regain the upper hand in the Dallas rivalry.

Astoundingly, while the Sooners incurred a four-loss season in 2005, many of the fans were already demanding Stoops's ouster. Stoops was sentenced to death by blogging. Postings that read: "Give Stoops a break. He lost all that talent to the NFL," to which somebody responded, "Hell, Wal-Mart loses good people every day, and it doesn't seem to slow *them* down." Somebody else claimed that Bob Stoops couldn't carry Barry Switzer's jock-strap, and yet another blogger countered with, "Why would he want to, considering the places that thing's been?"

Oklahoma football fans cannot tolerate the concept of losing. J. W. Whitworth, way back in the Bud Wilkinson era, was coaching at Oklahoma State (Oklahoma A&M in those days), and he said, "When Oklahoma loses a game, their fans become as mean as I wish my linemen were."

The Texas-USC Rose Bowl captured a television-viewing audience that topped the ratings in the fifty-five largest markets in the United States. Outside of Austin, the highest percentage of viewers tuned in to the game was in Oklahoma City. Everyone—well, let's say almost everyone—in Oklahoma was rooting for the Longhorns. Why? Because the Sooners' loyalists suddenly developed a kissy-face appreciation for the men in burnt orange and all of their modest and unassuming backers? Or because the Oklahomans saw the T-shirts some Texas fans wore to the game in Dallas that proclaimed, "You Can't Spell Cocksucker Without OU," and that cracked them up so they instantly wanted to root for the Horns?

Sober up. OU people were pulling for Texas for two reasons: One, if Texas didn't snap USC's thirty-four-game winning streak, the Trojans would then endanger OU's proud all-time streak of forty-seven victories in a row. And two, the Oklahomans realized that if Texas won, the probability was that Vince Young would join the NFL, and the Sooners had enjoyed their fill of seeing what the quarterback could do as a collegian.

Must have been a strange scene at those Rose Bowl game-watching parties throughout the state of Oklahoma. People were cheering for the Longhorns, all the while flashing the contemptuous upside-down Hook 'Em Horns sign. People overseas, none of whom knew anything about American football, watched the crowd shots at the Texas-OU game and thought that there was a lot of devil worship involved. After the Rose Bowl game, after Texas had won, people at the OU gatherings were saying things like, "Know why those TU fans wear orange shirts to the football games? So they won't have to change shirts when they go to work the next morning, picking up trash along the highway."

Texas and Oklahoma have played one hundred games, and the hundred-and-first might be the best one ever. OU quarterback Rhett Bomar is the second coming of Brett Favre and running back Adrian Peterson—he might not be a once-in-a-lifetime player like Vince Young, but he's a once-every-two-decades stallion. So the next installment of the Texas-OU series will attract a spectacle for which people *will* pay something like a grand to sit and watch in the end zone.

Yeah, and it'll be a majestic college football production. Heritage, though, and tradition are the elements that fuel this remarkable rivalry. The people who will cram into the old Cotton Bowl for the next renewal might be reminded that before there was this, there was that—*that* being the historical elements providing the substance and meaning to the series. So this book is a tribute to *that* . . . the people and the times coming together to produce a sporting event that involves so much skull-busting fury that it cannot be replicated.

2

Riot Night in Dallas

Like almost everything of value produced in the culture known as the United States of America, the Texas-OU football series got started big as a carnival attraction. The aeroplane. The motor car. Everything Thomas Edison ever invented. The hamburger. TV. These sorts of curious novelties caught on because of the mass exposure received at some city's world's fair or international exhibition.

The Texas-Oklahoma game was hardly a novelty but needed showroom exposure. The schools had been playing off and on since 1900, in that era when all of the players parted their hair straight down the middle. This notion of Texas-OU, it was a great concept but a little too off-Broadway in those early years. In 1929, the football game was added on a permanent basis as a crowd-pleasing attraction to the State Fair of Texas. The football game was scheduled as an adjunct to the fair's headline draw, a Wild West shoot-'em-up show.

They played the game in Fair Park Stadium (the Cotton Bowl wasn't built yet) to a standing room only crowd of 18,000. Texas won, 21–0; the entire event was a marvelous success; and the setting for the great football series was in place forever. What was also forever was almost everybody's life turning to ashes, which happened ten days after the game when the stock market collapsed. And the darkness crossed the land, spreading deeply into two generations. The offspring of that hard-times generation suffered, too. Nobody was hungry anymore but might as well have been, 'cause the old man was too cheap to let a kid buy a ten-cent comic book.

Nowhere was it worse than on the dust-choked prairies of the Sooner State, and those Dust Bowl Okies became the most celebrated down-and-outers in the history of American poverty. *The dawn came, but no day. In the gray sky a dim red circle that gave a little light, like dusk; and as that day advanced, the dusk slipped back toward darkness and the wind cried and whimpered over the fallen corn.*

Meanwhile, lyricist Richard Rodgers kept reminding them that, "Breadlines seemed less burdensome if one could sing and Armageddon couldn't threaten us if we kept on whistling 'Bye-Bye Blackbird.'" The gall.

Hard times didn't do much for the football, either. Texas, in particular, had slumped, so in Austin they launched the five-year Bible Plan to revive the program, that being Dana X. Bible, ex–Texas Aggies coach, by way of Nebraska. By 1941, Bible had advanced the program to the point that *Life* magazine, the premier media product in the nation at the time, devoted a cover story to the Longhorns. The cover itself consisted of simple head shots of fourteen Longhorns—mostly rodeo faces, lean and tough. The story talked about how the University of Texas had grown from a forlorn community of shacks into the "biggest, richest university in the South." That happened when an underground lake of oil was found beneath some semidesert acreage that had been deeded to the school. And—Texans being Texans—the UT people built the thirty-two-story tower library, with its two-million-volume capacity, and went out and bought a world-famous collection of Robert Browning, a page from the Gutenberg Bible, a first folio of Shakespeare, original manuscripts of Byron and Tennyson, and the world's largest drum.

Well, the drum came later, but the school was the beneficiary of some oil-drunk Texans like the guy in Sherman, Texas, who donated a fortune to the school for the purpose of building a telescope so strong that he could peer through the gates of heaven and see who is inside. Thus, the McDonald Observatory, near Fort Davis. The UT spread in *Life* appeared in the November 17 issue, when Texas fans and college fans across America figured that the Longhorns were heading to Pasadena for the Rose Bowl, the granddaddy of them all, as it was regarded in those times. Then a funny thing happened to the Longhorns on the way to the Rose Bowl. They tied Baylor and then lost to Texas Christian University. Turns out fate had prearranged that nobody was going to Pasadena anyway. A month after the Longhorns appeared in *Life,* the magazine cover consisted of a black-and-white photo of an American flag. The nation was at war, and after Pearl Harbor, they played the 1942 Rose Bowl game in Durham, North Carolina.

The United States and its allies won that war, by the way. Our enemies never had a chance from the opening kickoff, really. The Japanese naval commander, Admiral Yamamoto, had visited the East Texas oil fields, where the skyline of eternal derricks stretched to the horizon and beyond, way off into Oklahoma. Yamamoto went home to Japan and said, "Don't do this," but they did it anyway.

And this gets us rapidly to the gist of the story, because the oil boom in Oklahoma and Texas was what put the kick into this football series, and when it cranked up good at the end of World War II, nothing much could match it. This had become a petroleum-based rivalry, born of the spirit and reckless élan that characterized the lords of the oil patch, who were imbued with a brashness of stride that one might see in a man leaving the dice table with his pockets full . . . the natural cool that comes from cash flow.

The pathway to prosperity and happiness in the world was chained to three fundamentals:

Get up early.

Work hard.

Find oil.

Those other Red State college football rivals, down in Dixie and throughout the Midwest, well . . . with all due respect, World War II wasn't fought over pork bellies; the Nazis didn't lose because they ran out of cotton; and the Japanese didn't surrender because all of a sudden sweet potatoes were in short supply. That oil economy breathed a postwar fire, and places like Ponca City, where Conoco had its operation, became vibrant and alive. In Bartlesville, home of Phillips Petroleum, Frank Lloyd Wright was hired to design an office building, a nice twelve-story gem. Phillips 66 sponsored an amateur basketball team that could beat most colleges. According to a person familiar with the history, "They reached out to culture . . . and athletics."

The state of Oklahoma had arisen again, and the Sooners football team, in the way that it had begun to play, embodied the spirit of a proud people. Oklahoma embraced the football team as if every touchdown could avenge the agonies of the recent past. Now the people's natural urge, when the dice were smoking, was to look toward larger conquests. And, God, what better adversary than Texas, land of great bravado, land of the loud. The great leering giant. Tyrannosaurus Tex. Certain Sooners felt that in the world's view, Texas was the Lone Ranger and Oklahoma was Tonto, and that had to stop.

Those Oklahomans, they hadn't whipped hard times and our enemies overseas by attending candlelight vigils, praying for moist clouds and peace. Men like these, as head-on as they approach the world, tend to develop large appetites. Large and lustful. No gathering place on the planet for partaking in the Whiskey Feud—this Texas-OU Testosterone Bowl—could have been more welcoming than Dallas, the wind-blown temptress of the great southern plain. Kingdom Cum.

Forget the image that some people have of Dallas as this bastion of uptight Baptist intolerance. Nonsense. After Jack Ruby got sentenced to die in the Texas electric chair, to ride Old Sparky (that got overturned, most people forget), his lawyer, Melvin Belli, called Dallas "the city of hate." C'mon. Give it a rest. People don't come pouring into Dallas and its pulsing neon streets to spend their money on hate. Harry Hines Boulevard, which winds out of downtown Dallas northwesterly for about ten miles, is to Dallas as the Mississippi River is to St. Louis. Taverns, smelling of Lysol and cigarette smoke that hangs in the air thick as cotton candy, line the boulevard. Next door are always places where the rooms come with little sheds where a gentleman can conceal his automobile. I've been around this place a long time, and I can tell you that Dallas is okay, and around the clock the streets are alive with people loaded on everything from acid to Zoloft. Jimmie Dale Gilmore, in his song "Have You Ever Seen Dallas from a DC-9 at Night," says that "Dallas is a rich man with a death wish in his eye."

More people see Dallas as something else . . . a pretty woman who likes for people to buy her nice things.

Oklahoma's postwar football fans, the first regiments of the red invaders of October, came to Dallas boiling with the intent to show up and be somebody. The beginning chapters and verses from the Book of Texodus tell us that at first things were good, and then the spirit of the people of the land took over. Before long, and for decades then to come, anybody staying downtown the night before the Texas-OU game would drift off to sleep to the lullaby of sirens and shattering glass.

"In the early 1950s, they had a Texas-OU dance at the convention center, and there was a big pep rally. The Texas cheerleaders would climb up on the overhang in front of the Adolphus. Then the parties that involved the students in town for the game, those moved out of downtown, and that was when the idiots began to take over the streets. By 1952, the Dallas police were placed on a riot alert status the Friday night before the game.

"And that's what it was. Riot night in Dallas."

The speaker is Jim Bowles, sheriff of Dallas County for more than two decades, until he retired. Actually, he was retired by the voters, done in finally by the poison fangs of politics in 2004. He's not a damn bit happy about that now, and the memories of the early Texas-OU street wars, back when Bowles was a Dallas police officer, don't lighten his spirits at all. "You know . . . you come out of the Depression and all that meant, the values . . . and then you watch those lunatics . . . and you wonder what in the *hell* drives people to join the mob and carry on like a crazy, destructive madman and . . . at first, the people who got arrested had tickets to the game, and we let them out early. And then, nobody had tickets. . . . Damn thugs, all they did was prove that you don't have to be an Okie to be an idiot . . . Sol's Turf Bar on Commerce was the first place to board up his windows by Friday noon . . . but by 1959 you could drive down the busiest streets of downtown Dallas, before that weekend, and all of the businesses and all of the store fronts looked like they were ready for a hurricane . . . I can tell you for sure that Stanley Marcus, if he didn't want the game moved out of Dallas, he damn sure wanted that Friday-night scene moved away from downtown. Put a little pressure on to get that done. He was afraid the mob would smash in his show windows and assault the mannequin . . . no, hell no, there wasn't anything funny about working the streets on Texas-OU weekend. The last person I arrested was the son of an astronaut."

Another retired police officer told me that most of the Texas-OU revelers on Football Eve, participants in the fetish dance celebrating the night that America goes wrong, would ordinarily be spending their Friday evening driving their pickups through Reverchon Park and throwing lug nuts at the "queers."

I confess that having lived in this area during the prime years of this Million Man March of Psychos, I never, not once, came anywhere near the primeval echoes from downtown Dallas. Heard stories. The best one came from a guy who was set loose on the streets wearing a dress as part of a fraternity hazing event. He went to North Texas State. "The problem wasn't the dress. The problem was that I got arrested facedown in the gutter. And when I passed out again in the tank, some motherfucker set my hair on fire." He points at a little notchlike disfiguration at the top of his forehead, a memento of his Texas-OU night.

Jay Cronley—the son of John Cronley, columnist for *The Daily Oklahoman*—wrote a terrific story that appeared in *Playboy* detailing the horrors that awaited the naifs who dared the streets. Cronley was an OU student and wrote that "the most adroit Texan" he'd ever seen leaped upon the hood of his car and wrote "fuck oklahoma" across the windshield with shoe polish, but wrote it backward so the people inside could read it. Then somebody insulted Cronley's date, and he reluctantly got from his car to defend the honor of his lady. Cronley handed his new sport coat to an onlooker, took a punch in the nose, and then watched the onlooker as he took off running with the coat.

Refuge from the savagery of the Dallas streets was available for the football visitor at the Adolphus and Baker hotels, the landmarks on Commerce Street. Most notably, the Adolphus still stands and operates. The hotel opened in 1912 ("Dallas gazed at the impact of her beauty, and everything else on the horizon seemed dwarfed and provincial") and was named after Adolphus Busch, the brewery baron. Every person of celebrity consequence in American life has stayed there since the opening.

Not every one, obviously. Some people such as Elvis preferred to stay at the homes of friends. But Caruso and Valentino. Amelia Earhart, FDR, and the list just goes on forever. When Harry Truman, and that was when he was actually the president, visited the Adolphus, the hotel sent up a complimentary bottle of scotch and a bottle of bourbon. Give 'em Hell Harry called down, thanked the hotel, and wondered if he couldn't trade the bottle of scotch for another bottle of bourbon. In 1992, Her Royal Highness Queen Elizabeth II stayed the night. During her visit, she appeared at some highfalutin ceremony at the Hall of State, which is a museum at Fair Park. There she was greeted by some local protestors. No one was certain what they were protesting, probably they themselves didn't know, but they stood in unison and chanted, "The queen is a bitch! The queen is a bitch!"

Architects designed the building in the style of the École des Beaux-Arts, with a bronze and slate mansard roof and a façade decorated with French Renaissance features in relief. There was only one other hotel in the region that came close to approaching the grandeur of the Adolphus, that being the Jackson Hotel at Tenth and Main Street in Fort Worth. Rooms were available for $5.50, and even though they were available for only about twenty minutes, you wouldn't believe the amenities.

So it's amazing to visualize a facility with the formal pomp and elegance of the Adolphus serving once a year as command central to the people-gone-berserk Texas-Oklahoma football weekend. That's the way it happened. In the words of a hotel historian: "Occasionally, serious efforts were made to discourage the tide of college students surging up into the hotel and sweeping out onto the balconies. Sometimes, the situation seemed to be hopeless, with the lobby covered with debris and glass."

The hotel borrowed the services of Bill Bass, a seven-foot-tall black man and famed doorman at the La Tunisia Restaurant; dressed him in a top hat and paid him to whap folks on the head who tried to enter the hotel without a key. He would suggest, "Look, why don't you go on to some other place."

For ten years, OU grad Clark Chambers and a friend would rent the top-floor Presidential Suite at the Adolphus for the big weekend. What he remembers is Gatsby-esque. "Sometimes we would throw whiskey bottles and beer cans off the balconies, but there was a ledge beneath us, and you couldn't see anything land on the street. The Presidential Suite had its own private elevator that ran straight to the lobby, and sometimes folks would wind up in our suite by mistake. The suite had three bedrooms and a big living room. On Saturday morning, I would wake up and the floor would be strewn with broken glass and passed-out bodies, people I'd never seen before and would never see again."

Clark Chambers typifies the OU Man of his generation. Chambers made a lot of money and remained close to the football program. He remembers sitting in Barry Switzer's office while the coach was showing a film of Billy Sims running around in a high school game in East Texas. Chambers says that his life has been successful enough, "except matrimonially." His three marriages, combined, lasted about the length of an episode of *Bonanza*. The theme is consistent here. Plenty of men are like Clark Chambers.

What they did was go to Dallas for the football weekend

and inhale the spectacle, and it was love at first sight. These guys had the hots for a football game, but finally the wife would catch on, and it came down to "Okay, it's going to be *it* or me. Make up your mind." And the battle over community property would begin. These were tough fights, but never as intense as the Texas-OU fixation, the reason they were hiring lawyers in the first place. It's a miracle that nobody's ever sued the Texas-OU game for alienation of affection or intentional infliction of emotional distress. Old and alone now, many of them, these hard-core Texas-OU football fiends wake up each day singing the ditty that goes, "If I can't live without you, then how come I ain't dead?" Clark Chambers, who lives in Dallas and is a wine consultant, recalls the nocturnal butchery that happened in that Presidential Suite at the Adolphus and says, "The weekend was a situation, didn't matter who you were, that when you came to Dallas on that weekend, you weren't just entitled, you were obligated to get twice as drunk as you ever got at home. If you didn't, your team might lose. Still, what I cannot figure out is why so many glasses got broken, but they did. Room service kept bringing new ones up in racks."

The Saturday encounter in the Cotton Bowl—the Red versus the Burnt Orange, no pastel shadings to this rivalry—would produce a loser. One was never certain which one would partake of the stale beer of defeat. Friday night, though, there was always one big loser, every year: the Ten Commandments. God, the morning after, and the dreadful coming-of-game-day dawn.

I began to waken very early in the morning shaking violently. A tumbler full of gin followed by a half-dozen bottles of beer would be required if I were to eat any breakfast. Nevertheless, I still thought I could control the situation.

The most enduring descriptions of the Friday-night awfulness entail versions of television sets flying down from the windows of the Adolphus and the Baker. The sightings have not met with official verification from responsible authorities. A few old ex-cops, and that includes former Sheriff Bowles, can confirm furniture, including a sofa, and people falling from the hotel windows and balconies, but no TVs. That contradicts many-told tales of the RCAs and Philcos coming down like hailstones in April.

So the vision of the falling television enters the same realm as the mysterious Marfa Lights, phantom illuminations that appear along the barren mountainsides in the farthest reaches of West Texas. I know two people who have actually witnessed the Marfa Lights, eerie phosphorescent flashes on the mountain. One said the show was worth it, the other described the lights as small, wavering, and faint. A helluva disappointment, really. Anybody who's really seen a television hit the Dallas pavement probably didn't feel such a letdown.

The closest eyewitness account of any flying television sets—since official law enforcement people and the media let me down—comes from Dallas resident Chris Koehler. This is his statement:

> *I grew up in Rhode Island and was rather a proper New Englander. When I was eighteen, my father came to Dallas on a business trip and asked me to accompany him. And I did, wanting to see what Texas was like. The trip happened to coincide with the Texas-OU weekend, 1965.*
>
> *We stayed at the Baker Hotel and watched the action on the sidewalk from our window. I was scared to go down there. Too wild. The people staying in the*

Baker were outrageously drunk. I did not physically see a television set come out of a window and crash on the street, but I heard it hit the street, and saw people gathered around down there, gaping at the wreckage and pointing up at the hotel. I hoped that my father would pass out so I could go down to the street. But he never did. It was overwhelming. I knew then that Dallas had something special going for it and made up my mind right then and there that I wanted to spend the rest of my life here. And I pretty much have.

Chris Koehler is of an age where he's got no reason to be out telling a bunch of lies.

3

The Smiling Master

Next to playing Russian roulette with a shotgun, one could scarcely conceive a game more unhealthy and potentially damaging to every tooth, bone, tendon, and gut-string in the human body than American football. For the participants, almost every play is like skiing into a tree. Out here on the raw plains, breeding grounds for oh-so-many of the essential characters on the grand stage of the Texas-OU October series, they all learned young about the realities of the sport. Football is not a contact sport. Dancing is a contact sport. Football is a collision sport. Take twenty-two big, fast muthahs who are not exactly testosteronally challenged, put 'em out on a one-and-a-half-acre lot, and let 'em run into one another, fast as they can, head-on, play after play after play. The helmet, that's a weapon, not a protective device. Ram your hat under the other guy's face mask and open his chin up like a new supermarket. And then, on the very next play, while the other guy is getting back into his stance, bleeding all over his jersey, you stomp his hand with your cleats and rake it across the turf.

Most every snap, you're involved in a one-second alley fight. Wonder what they say in the huddle in these schoolboy games?

"Jodie, you go long. Ever'body else try to whup somebody's ass. On three."

So out here on the flat frontier, a game like that seemed as natural a thing to do as sunbathe in Pago Pago. Not long after the Civil War, about the same time football was emerging as a college lad's alternative to dueling, the territory that spawned the Texas-OU gridiron prototype was a bloodbath. Comanche and Kiowa discouraged early Texas tourism by murdering settlers at a rate of what turned out to be nineteen per mile, from Fort Worth westward, halfway to El Paso. Chopped 'em to pieces and fed 'em to the dogs. Tied people to wagon wheels and roasted 'em over mesquite coals. But the Texas newcomers, armed, dangerous, and not at all above some scalp-taking of their own, killed some Indians, them and the Mexicans, which was their intent before they ever left home in the first place. Then, after almost everybody was dead and the treaties were signed, the Indians and pioneers began to comingle, sharing and exchanging cultural facets such as fashion trends. Cross-breeding became widespread and produced the Scots-Irish-Comanche hybrid that was fast, ferocious, and adventuresome. Sometimes a perfect storm would occur, DNA-wise, and then you'd have a helluva halfback on your hands.

Before football was introduced into the territory around Texas's Brazos River and beyond, spectator sports consisted of Spartan-like competitions such as the one concocted by gunfighter Clay Allison. That involved Allison and his adversary digging a grave, climbing in, and participating in a knife fight, while naked, with the last man alive being declared the winner. Had Clay Allison come along at a later time, his natural flair for aggression would have been nicely suited for a middle linebacker, for either Texas or OU.

People in that territory were, as the locals like to say, crazier than a shit-house rat. Wichita Falls, Texas, which supplied a pipeline of football players to both the Texas and OU teams, stands at the geographic center of the Red River badlands. When the Texas legislature offered the town its choice to be the locale for either Texas Tech University or a state mental hospital, the city fathers of Wichita Falls studied the needs of the area populous and opted for the madhouse.

So a sport as barbaric as football would naturally appeal to the innate primeval passions and competitive instincts of those people daring enough to venture into the territory. Terrific spectator appeal, of course. Custer's Last Stand with a halftime show.

By age sixteen, all of these kids of the region who played football had been exposed to sadistic practices . . . "You're not hurt! Git back out thar, you gutless chickenshit!" . . . and listened to the standard-issue pregame motivational message, delivered likely as not by a man who's got a nineteen-and-a-half-inch neck and a bad marriage. Coach would say, "Ya' know, twenty, thirty years from tonight, you might look back on this game. You won't remember the final score, might not even remember if we won the game. Here's what I'd like for you to remember, though. I'd like it if you remember going out there and hittin' those guys and keepin' on hittin' 'em until buttermilk comes outta their ears. So let's go out there and break somebody's gah-damn neck.

"Now, Sheffield, lead us in the Lord's Prayer."

"Uh . . . uh . . . the Lord is my shepherd . . ."

"Gah-damn! That ain't it! What the hell's the matter with you, Sheffield?"

Prototypical football coaches maintained a demeanor and style usually associated with men who oversee prison road gangs, those jovial fellows who sit on horseback, wearing mirrored sunglasses and holding rifles. If not a prison guard, then perhaps a strike buster for the coal mining industry.

Then Bud Wilkinson took charge at the University of Oklahoma, shattering every perceived image of the football coach that was in place when he got the job in Norman in 1947. Bud, movie-star handsome with wavy hair and sparkling eyes, was smooth, charming, poised, articulate. He did not chew tobacco and could complete a sentence without saying the F word. Bud seldom raised his voice, and never in anger, and he did not motivate through intimidation. Nobody in this part of the world had ever seen such a person so stylish and sleek, particularly working as a football coach. "Bud always looked like he'd stepped right out of the barbershop," an envious Bear Bryant would declare. "I wish I had his class."

Wilkinson had grown up in Minneapolis, which is why he didn't talk with a twang (he played on a neighborhood football team, the 50th Street Tigers, quarterbacked by future women's golf great Patty Berg). Bud played on national championship football teams at Minnesota under Bernie Bierman, then entered coaching. During the war, he coached under Don Faurot at Iowa Pre-Flight, where he learned the most intimate details of the option-oriented Split-T offense. Jim Tatum hired Wilkinson as an assistant at OU, and when Tatum departed to coach the Maryland Terps, Wilkinson was elevated to the Sooners' head coach. From that day forward, the state of Oklahoma would experience a spiritual rebirth via football.

When Rodgers and Hammerstein wrote the hit musical that was geared to elevate the morale of those hearty souls who braved the darkest hours of the Dust Bowl doom, they should have hired Bud Wilkinson to choreograph the production. Bud's Split-T attack, so awesome and swift, operated with a flair and panache that embodied the famous Oklahoma wind that "comes sweeping down the plain." Built for speed—the Oklahoma teams looked streamlined in their low-cut football shoes—Wilkinson's teams were ideal for showcasing on television.

"A thunderstorm on the prairie, as upon the ocean, derives grandeur and sublimity from the wild and boundless waste over which it rages and bellows." That, according to Washington Irving, but the thunderstorm of the prairie was what Wilkinson introduced to the realm of college football. After he'd blueprinted the schematic for the unstoppable Split-T assault, Wilkinson and his assistant, Gomer Jones, then designed the defense that would shut it down. The so-called Oklahoma defense, aka the five-four Okie, was soon installed as the boilerplate defensive scheme for every high school football coach west of the Mississippi.

Wilkinson, the smiling master, employed Norman Vincent Peale's power of positive thinking to stoke the machine. One of his stars from the early 1950s, Billy Pricer, would recall, "You'd feel like quitting school and joining the French Foreign Legion. Then you'd talk to Bud for fifteen minutes and come out of his office singing 'Boomer Sooner' and thinking you owned half of the university."

Bud was committed to putting teams on the field that were populated by players who defied the popular image of the football player as a toothless, ignorant jock. Wilkinson was a fanatic for preparation. "If you have the will to prepare, the will to win will take care of itself," he told the players. Once the players were indeed prepared, it was up to them to think on their feet as they implemented Wilkinson's game plans, which were as meticulously tailored as the suits he wore. "Bud was real demanding when it came to knowing what to do, when to do it, and how to do it," said one of his all-American linemen, J. D. Roberts. The football player prone to mental lapses wouldn't find himself on the field on Saturday. "The fact that our men believe they can use their brains to defeat a physically superior opponent pays dividends you can't reckon with," Bud would say.

Wilkinson had the living ideal of that kind of competitor in his quarterback, Darrell Royal—wiry, compact, and bright. Not only did Darrell maintain the quick-thinking capacity to run Wilkinson's precision offensive, with its nanosecond timing; he also played defense. The fact that Royal intercepted seventeen passes in his four seasons at OU stands as an irrefutable testimonial to his rare gift of anticipation. Royal was a product of Hollis, Oklahoma, which sits right at the elbow of the Red River where it turns down from the Texas and Oklahoma panhandles. People who choose to exist on those barren flatlands are plumb loco. This landscape is known as Tornado Alley. God kept bringing these killer twisters along the river, thinking the people would take the hint and move on. But they never did. It is well documented that the Red River no-man's-land was populated by a breed of personality that expressed itself in behavioral extremes. A popular story from a village in the region tells of the kindly aunt who offered to purchase a shotgun for her nephew's eighteenth birthday on the stipulation that he memorize the entire Old Testament within six months. The boy accomplished that, and when he received the weapon, he used it to blow his aunt's head off. People around the town joked that if the woman had only insisted that the boy commit the entire Bible to memory, she would have lasted out the year.

People and events like that were as commonplace as rattlesnakes and tumbleweeds out there where Darrell Royal played high school sports and watched the way his elders behaved. That Oklahoma outback was no place for sissies, and the survival traits that Royal inherited amid rough terrain would serve him in greater stead than his wits when it came to the gridiron.

Wilkinson understood that. Beyond the strategy and the perfection of execution, this sport was, remember, a playground of brutality. Bud defined it nicely: "Football, in its purest form, is a physical fight. As in any fight, if you don't want to fight, it's impossible to win." Wilkinson knew something else. Some people across the Red River, in the enemy territory of Texas, some of those people really liked to fight, and they were good at it. You could stand in any saloon and find some sawed-off little pistol-packing hyena talking about how to whip a man twice his size. "Jist grab him by his ear, lift your feet off the ground, and let gravity do all the work. Peel his goddamn ear right off his head, and then, he's so freaked out about his ear, all he can do is stand there while you stomp the pig shit out of him." Sickeningly, you do see a lot of one-eared big guys in West Texas.

But people from this area, where they could serve fried tarantula in the diners and call it calamari, *did* have the stomach for the good fight, and as far as Bud Wilkinson was concerned, he couldn't have enough of those folks on a football team. So Wilkinson began importing Texas-bred talent on a wholesale basis. Any Oklahoma loyalist who might resent or distrust the player imported from the fatherland of self-congratulation and gluttony, that being Texas, might have been reminded that many of the children of settlers abducted by the Native American tribes became damn good Indians, and many a battle chief and warrior brave were of the white persuasion.

Realistically, winning what was then the Big Six Conference was Wilkinson's stated objective when he took charge, but the notion of whipping Texas, down in Dallas, was Bud's focus right away. So what could be more fun than going to Dallas and beating the Texas team with home-state people who didn't think enough of the Austin program and left for Soonerville, where they played real football?

Oh, what a setting Dallas would provide for invading Oklahomans, loud and proud. The State Fair of Texas was the largest exhibition of its kind in the entire solar system, of course. Where else, as you approached the stadium for a hugely important football game, would you encounter Howard, the nine-legged man; Beatrice, the amazing fifteen-hundred-pound blimp woman; and tiny little Terry, the human anchovy? And that wasn't on the carnival midway, either. Those were fairgoers just off the church bus from Gainesville. Now, for a quarter, you got to see the real thing, the "martha-dyte she-man" who was equipped, it told us, with, you know, one of each.

The fairground was alive with delightfully aromatic culinary atrocities, and the rickety wooden roller coaster that would help you puke the food back up, if you were so inclined. The fairground specialty was the mandatory Fletcher's Corny Dog—hot dog on a stick, coated in thick cornbread batter and deep fried. The Automobile Building was a huge draw. All of that year's new models, revolving on big turntables, cars with big fins over the rear bumpers, and real-life professional models standing next to the big silver and teal Buick Roadmaster sedan, avoiding eye contact with the yokels.

Despite the sensory overstimuli that the fair attractions imposed, the real catalyst that made the Texas-OU spectacle so vibrantly ingenious was the stadium itself, the Cotton Bowl. The gray concrete colossus is an acoustic marvel. With the upper decks built directly atop the lower stands and not recessed back, the shouts of the fans cascade down onto the field, so that the sound on the floor of the stadium, when it's full and rocking, becomes overwhelming. So the noise level on the ground begets new levels of energy from the football players, which then causes the people in the stands to howl that much louder, and a cyclonic convergence takes place inside the quaking arena. That's why the Rolling Stones like to play the Cotton Bowl, and the greatest move in the history of the stadium happened in 1956, at the State Fair, when Elvis Presley kicked that pelvis of his into Powerglide, and the king hunched his way from the fifty-yard line all the way down to the thirty-five, while the people screamed.

They didn't generate the noise of the 1948 Oklahoma crowd, though, when they beat the Longhorns, 20–14, winning the game in Dallas for the first time in nine years. Two future coaches of note had been on the field that day—Royal and the man playing fullback for the Longhorns, Tom Landry. After the clock ran down to 0:00 and the Sooners had hung on, hysteria reigned and Bud Wilkinson's legions, having finally severed the head of the orange dragon, would surge into the national limelight. The Sooners fan base developed a fascination with the program that became insatiable. The OU alums and supporters throughout the state adored Wilkinson and what he was accomplishing. It was the victory over their arrogant antagonists, the smirking Texans, that seared the Sooners' soul. The needle was buried deep in the arm, the beat-the-hell-out-of-Texas opiate surged into the blood supply, and the OU faithful were hooked, good and forever.

After Oklahoma captured the national title, topping both the Associated Press and United Press International polls at the completion of an unbeaten regular season in 1950, appreciative OU supporters took up a collection and bought Bud a new Cadillac. Also, as a token of esteem to the leader of the school, OU president George Cross, they presented him with a fine new cigarette lighter, suitably engraved for the occasion.

In 1952, halfback Billy Vessels had won the Heisman Trophy, but by 1953 Vessels was gone. Wilkinson was also undecided on who'd be his quarterback at the beginning of the 1953 season. OU lost its opener to Notre Dame; and the following game, it tied Pitt, 7–7. So the Sooners came to Dallas in a rare state of winlessness. The Longhorns, under coach Ed Price, were suspect as well. They lost their season opener for the second time in the history of the team, to Louisiana State University, in a game where Texas used four different quarterbacks. NBC carried the event on national television, and the Texas-OU fans in the Cotton Bowl filled the seats and overflowed into the aisles and onto the field. The throng would include U.S. Senator Lyndon Johnson, who was not a UT alum, and his wife, Lady Bird, who was.

They sat near Texas Lieutenant Governor Ben Ramsey, and they all moped throughout the afternoon. Wilkinson's team dominated the Longhorns. The final score was 19–14, but the Texas scores came when it was too late to matter. "I'm not getting a bit of fun out of this," said the lieutenant governor. "It's painful." Sooners fans stormed the field when it was over and ripped the wooden goalposts apart, breaking off pieces for souvenirs of the battle.

But the OU faithful, hearts resounding with joy while they were celebrating the 1953 victory over the Longhorns, had no idea of the fun that lay ahead. The victory started the greatest winning streak in college football, and the Sooners would not lose again for another forty-seven games.

During that amazing run of dominance, the Sooners experienced one genuine close call. That happened in Norman, against TCU, in 1954. The Horned Frogs were coached by the same man who would bedevil Darrell Royal: Abe Martin, who was pretty damn Lincolnesque in his look and manner. Martin took an almost gentle approach to preparing his teams after a kid died on him while he was coaching in high school.

Before the game, Wilkinson told his team that these Frogs from Fort Worth posed a clear danger, and he was right. OU had to rally to take a late 21–16 lead, and TCU came fighting back. On the last play of the game, quarterback Chuck Curtis threw a pass to the end and team captain Johnny Crouch, who appeared to catch it in the end zone. The official signaled "touchdown," and the Sooners were beaten and stunned until Crouch, schooled by Abe Martin to do the right thing, handed the ball to the official and said, "I didn't catch it, Ref. I trapped that ball." Another official, the field judge who'd had a better view of the play, concurred with Crouch, and the TD—and TCU's win—were canceled. Interestingly, the field judge was named Don Looney, and he had a son who would someday play football at Oklahoma. The following week, Crouch received a personal letter from the president of the United States, Ike himself, commending the Frogs end for his sportsmanship. (That '54 TCU team was no fluke and went on to beat Southern Cal and Penn State, although its season was ruined when the Frogs blew a 34–7 second-half lead against the Longhorns and wound up losing, 35–34, in Fort Worth.)

After that closest of possible close calls, the Sooners performed the greatest plains-states rampage since Bonnie and Clyde. In Dallas, the gap that separated OU from its ancient foe grew ever wider, and the 1956 contest turned out to be nothing other than a sixty-minute Sooners highlights film.

Wilkinson introduced gimmick plays from a "swinging gate" alignment, and the Sooners performed some sleight-of-hand artistry that elevated the entertainment value of the spectacle to a brand-new high. Halfbacks Tommy McDonald and Clendon Thomas ruled the field. When quarterback Jimmy Harris fumbled and was chased down for a twenty-nine-yard loss in the second quarter, on the next play the Sooners ran the "o-l-l-d Statue of Liberty play," with Thomas carrying the ball forty-four yards, and the slaughter was on. Oklahoma's 45–0 rout left the fans in both camps with the profound impression that Oklahoma might never lose to the Longhorns again in anybody's lifetime.

Jaw to Jaw

The 1956 football season at the University of Texas was nothing much more than a three-month-long lowlights film that was as somber, slow-paced, and futile as perhaps any in the gridiron past of the Austin campus. The Longhorns team wore goofy-looking helmets, which made them look like the crash dummies they had become; had a place-kicker named Bednarski who approached the ball from an angle (soccer-style, for God's sake); lost to the Texas Aggies in Austin for the first time since the Calvin Coolidge administration; and in fact lost every game on the schedule but one, a 7–6 win against Tulane. So after Texas lost to Oklahoma 45–0, the well-heeled wheelhorses from backstage who financed this dance determined that it must be about time for a coaching change.

Off-the-field discipline was in a declining state as well, and real folklore depicting Moore-Hill Hall, the jock dorm, as an animal house emanated from that era. Stories involving the dorm-life proclivities of twin tackles Wes and Will Wyman entailed details too hilariously extreme to be apocryphal.

The Wymans and others. An assistant coach and his wife were moved to the dorm to impede the lawlessness, into a suite directly beneath the Wyman boys' room. So Wes and Will took turns dangling each other by the ankles out of their window to peer upside down through the bathroom window beneath whenever they heard the coach's wife turn on the shower. So head coach Ed Price was fired and given a job as dean of student life. People who knew Price thought when the job change was enacted, he regarded the decision as a big relief.

Price's replacement—the source of statewide speculation—would not walk into any midsize renovation job. To do it right, the new guy would have to replace the whole damn foundation, since that was where the biggest cracks were, and that would get expensive. After the 1956 season, when Bud Wilkinson's Sooners had been so completely dominant, around Austin the notion of beating OU seemed as distant as a spaceship to Mars. On the great highway of life in the 1950s, the Oklahoma Sooners were driving a red Corvette while the women swooned, and the Longhorns remained behind the wheel of an orange Studebaker.

The OU game, huge as that was, loomed as only part of the challenge. It could have been argued that the 1956 Sooners team—although unbeaten and breathtakingly efficient—might finish fourth in the Southwest Conference. Yes, though the Sooners had beaten the Longhorns by the 45–zip margin in '56, TCU had gone OU one better—46–0. The Horned Frogs, under coach Abe Martin, had been stomping the hell out of everybody. That season, they beat Syracuse and Jim Brown in the Cotton Bowl. But TCU still hadn't really won its own conference. Bear Bryant's proud and unbeaten Texas Aggies, the Junction Boys, had won but were on probation and couldn't play in a bowl game. And both TCU and A&M were fortunate to have gotten past the Baylor Bears, which wound up getting invited to the Sugar Bowl and upsetting unbeaten Tennessee and its all-American single wing tailback, Johnny Majors.

And—on any given Saturday—SMU, Rice, and Arkansas were sitting there. Each was very capable of biting a big chunk out of some team's championship ambitions, and usually did. Now the new Longhorns would enter the league at the base of the totem pole, looking up at the faces of some mean and determined Southwest Conference hombres. This was a time when college football in the state of Texas was at its zenith. On football Saturdays, Kern Tips would entertain the audience with his completely unique play-by-play poetry, the lilting and cheerful radio voice of the Southwest Conference radio network, sponsored entirely by Humble Oil and Refinery. "Go to the games with Humble." In Kern Tips's audio world, placekickers didn't kick extra points—they made 7 out of 6. And those guys weren't diving for a loose football—they were playing "button, button—who's got the button?" And about once a quarter, somebody would run the "old dipsy-doodle." Nobody knew what that meant, but it sounded like a helluva lot. Everybody loved to listen to Kern Tips, but the Longhorns fans had not been hearing much of him lately, except for the Thanksgiving game against the Aggies, because the Horns were at the bottom of the conference and stuck with a second-string announcer, Ves Box. "The Longhorns are back to punt . . . it's a high, beautiful, booming spiral and—uh-oh! It's blocked!" Texas fans needed a coach who, if he couldn't lead the Longhorns to the Cotton Bowl, could at least lead them back to Kern Tips.

So who was the right man for this job? Frank Leahy, the fabled name from Notre Dame, was mentioned. Nobody knew how to beat Oklahoma anymore, it seemed, but Leahy had been the last man to do it, and that had been so long back, almost four years, that it didn't matter. How about Wilkinson's own chief of staff, Gomer Jones? Hell, if the Confederates had wanted a rematch against the Yankees, wouldn't it have made perfect sense to bring in William Tecumseh Sherman to turn things around? But Gomer was already the acknowledged successor to Wilkinson, whenever he might choose to leave.

Another name with strong Sooner origins was floating out there. Darrell Royal was the OU quarterback who beat the Longhorns in 1948 in the game that energized the galvanized Bud Wilkinson dynasty, when this new and avid postwar generation of Oklahoma fans learned how it felt to absolutely own the city of Dallas on Saturday night. Darrell fought the Longhorns like Audie Murphy fought the Huns that day. Darrell was still throwing up in the locker room when George Cross came to congratulate him.

So if nothing else, in Royal they would have a man who could coach against the Sooners and understand a thing or two about the program, how it worked and how Bud Wilkinson prepared for the Texas game. Royal was coaching at Washington when Texas offered him the job. It should be noted that the night before the interview that sealed the UT-Royal partnership, Darrell had gone to the movies and seen *Giant*. Evidently the film made an impact because a few years later somebody pointed out that his Texas quarterback couldn't run very fast. Royal said, "Yeah. And maybe Elizabeth Taylor can't sing."

The University of Texas decision to bring Royal, age thirty-three, down from the frozen northwest to Austin had to rank as the greatest hire in the entire history of American employment, even greater than the Grand Ole Opry signing on Hank Williams, given the outcome.

Royal stood out as a manager because he understood the esoteric nuances of effective communication. Week one on the job someone told Royal that one of the more desirable holdovers from the Ed Price regime was thinking about transferring.

"What should I tell him?"

"Tell him good-bye," says Royal.

John Steinbeck won a Pulitzer Prize writing about Darrell Royal, only the character was named Tom Joad. Without belaboring the point, Darrell Royal left Hollis, Oklahoma, and moved to California with his family. Right about the time Doye O'Dell was singing his hit song "Dear Oakie," which goes, in part, "Dear Oakie, if you see Arkie, tell 'im Tex's got a job for 'im out in Californ-ee . . . pickin' up prunes, squeezin' oil out of olives . . . Now, he'll be lucky if he finds a place to live . . . but there's orange juice fountains flowin' for those kids of his . . ."

This is a beautifully performed song, particularly for one with a mean-spirited lyric like that one. And then Texans wonder why certain Oklahomans seem to hold this grudge. Royal hitchhiked back to Oklahoma because he wanted to play football in Hollis. What came of that was a man not carrying any grudges but a hard pragmatism etched in the teachings of survival with honor. He'd jump out of the Goodyear Blimp before he would compromise a principle. Tom Joad, the hero in *The Grapes of Wrath*, griped to his brother Al, after it's evident Al let the oil get too low and burned up the motor on the truck, on the cruel highway heading west.

"I kep' plenty oil in," Al complained.

"Well, it jus' didn' get to her. Drie'n a bitch monkey now. Well, there's nothing to do but tear her out. Look, I'll pull ahead and find a flat place to stop."

That might as well have been Darrell Royal in the locker room after he'd lost to Arkansas or somebody. Too late for excuses. Face the realities like they were. And that's the essence of the successful coach over the rigors of the season, finding a flat place to stop and regroup.

After taking over the Longhorns, Royal saw his immediate mission was to put a stop to the Sooners. The Horned Frogs and Aggies were averaging more than forty points a game.

Royal's team would tackle and play defense. It's defense that wins the games. "If worms had pistols, birds wouldn't eat them," said Royal.

An archconservative in his football views, Royal adhered to the theology of Woody Hayes, who was telling people that he hoped he never recruited a great passer. Great passes win some specular victories, Hayes believed, but they never win championships. Royal's thinking on the matter was that three things can happen when you throw forward passes, and two of them are bad.

Royal's austerity-embracing ideologies spilled over into areas like uniforms. This was a time when teams, SMU notably, were spiffing up their look, with those UCLA stripes running vertically across the shoulders coming into style, particularly among the high schools. "We're not going to candy this thing up," Royal said. "These are work clothes." Talk about no frills. On the road, in particular. Plain white helmet, plain white jersey, plain white pants, no stripes, no nothing. When the Longhorns took the field, you weren't sure whether they were there to play a football game or paint the stadium.

But that was Royal's taste, and interestingly, after Texas had beaten Southern Cal a couple of generations later, some fashion commentator was going on about the "appeal of the stylistic simplicity of that mostly-all-white look" and how it got high marks for product recognition. In 1962, Royal mandated a return to the Longhorns' burnt-orange home jerseys. It wasn't because Christian Dior had called with a suggestion. Royal didn't care how they looked. He figured that the football might be easier to conceal against the background of the darker-colored jersey.

Everything that Royal implemented when he arrived was strictly based on his plow-the-straight-row viewpoint on football and life. The excesses of dorm life at Moore-Hill were extinguished. "Without supervision, the inmates will take over the asylum, and that took place," says a player familiar with the pre-Royal era. "Those were the days. And as soon as the new staff arrived, those days were over."

Royal assigned assistant coach Jim Pittman to oversee dormitory discipline. Some ex-Longhorns remember walking toward Moore-Hill Hall after morning classes and seeing clothes fluttering from a third-floor window. A player had busted up his room—and his window—in a dorm fight, and now Pittman was heaving his belongings out the same window while the player left for good out the front door. Jim Pittman had a face that made G.I. Joe look like Liberace, and his "my way or the highway" approach was unbendable. When Pittman became the head coach at TCU in 1971, the first thing he did was run off four of his best players because they refused to shave off their mustaches. That quartet included defensive back Ray Rhodes, who later became head coach of the Philadelphia Eagles and Green Bay Packers.

In the new Royal regime in Austin, much of the team's hardening process was overseen by Frank Medina—"a little bitty, short Indian"—who was not only the trainer but the conditioning coach as well. He drove the players like sled dogs in his off-season conditioning workouts . . . the infamous Medina Sessions . . . that included punching the heavy bag and skipping rope, hours on end. Medina was carrying Royal's mandate. You have to be able to whip Rocky Marciano before you can realistically figure to go up to Dallas and whip OU.

Medina's rehab tyrannies remain the stuff of whispered legend. Players fled the training area rather than endure the screams of linebacker-fullback Don Allen, as he attempted a comeback after knee surgery, with little Medina overseeing the therapy. To strengthen surgically repaired weight-bearing joints, Medina would drive the healing player to Georgetown, thirty miles north of Austin, drop him off and have him walk back to town. Royal entrusted Medina with teaching the players deportment as well. Medina taught the freshmen how they ought to look when they went to class and how to clean up their rooms.

In spring 1957, practice took on a feeling of urgency under the regime. Royal was a hands-on coach, particularly with his quarterbacks, and would take snaps himself and run behind the line to demonstrate the technique that he wanted, that he demanded. Correct execution of all phases of the kicking game was an almost manic obsession. In these workouts, Royal and his staff charted the course of each player's approach to the sessions. "A boy shows how much he wants to play in the spring when it's tough, and in two-a-days when it's hot and tough," Royal would tell people. "I don't count on the boy who waits until October, when it's cool and fun, and then decides he wants to play. He might be better than three guys in front of him, but I know those three won't change their minds in the fourth quarter."

Royal beat the Georgia Bulldogs in his Longhorn debut. The team captains were Robert E. Lee for Texas and Jefferson Davis for Georgia. And while Royal based his entire coaching ethic on the hard-labor manifesto of persons familiar with the contours of the pipe wrench and the plow, his first-ever starting quarterback at Texas was Walter Fondren, the product of a family in Houston that has libraries named after it.

In October the Soviets launched their famous *Sputnik* spacecraft, but the big story of the month, the real stunner, was that for the first time in three years, the Longhorns scored a touchdown against the Sooners and actually led for a while before becoming Victim Forty-Three in the Oklahoma winning streak. OU won, 21–7.

The 1957 Longhorns weren't world-beaters, but they beat the two best teams in the Southwest Conference, Jess Neely's Rice Owls, who played in the Cotton Bowl, and more importantly to Texas fans, the Texas Aggies. That would mark Bear Bryant's last regular-season game in College Station. He was leaving for Alabama and immortality. Texas loyalists, of course, were relieved to see Bear go.

So the 1958 season dawned with the most elevated expectations that the Horns faithful had seen since the earliest part of the decade, and the team responded to the challenge. Texas beat Georgia, Tulane, and Texas Tech and drove into Dallas. OU's winning streak had ended, finally. Notre Dame had finished it off in November 1957, in Norman, 7–0. And afterward, Monte Stickles, the Irish captain, said the damndest thing: "There's an awful lot of animosity against Catholics in this state. Oklahoma is just three percent Catholic. When we went to our pregame mass Saturday morning, there were these Mexican kids, just begging us to win so they wouldn't have to put up with all that crap for so long. If we beat Oklahoma, maybe it would make things easier for Catholics in the state."

So the implication was that it had taken a papal mandate to end the Sooners' forty-seven-game victory run. But if the Longhorns were counting on any aid from the Vatican as well, those hopes were dashed on the Wednesday prior to the 1958 OU game. Pope Pius XII died, and Texas was on its own. And the 1958 Sooners looked every bit as menacing as in previous editions on the week of the game. Wilkinson's offense showed a new and daring presentation. Against West Virginia, OU won 47–14 using what some writer had termed "a weird assortment of flankers and spread formations." A scout for the Oregon Ducks, OU's upcoming opponent, said, "They'll never believe me back home. They'll never believe me. Len Casanova [head coach] will swear I was drunk." Texas assistant coach Mike Campbell dubbed the new Sooner offense the "flank 'em and fly."

Bud Wilkinson's sudden bent for the razzle-dazzle was not the focal point of Royal's pregame concern. Royal had been a product of the Wilkinson system, too, remember, and he knew this preparing for Dallas. "The only way anybody is going to beat Oklahoma is to go in there and whip 'em jaw to jaw. Any team that would play Oklahoma timidly would be humiliated," Royal declared. "They get a yellow dog running downhill, and they'll strap him real good." And Royal refused to rule out the notion that his team might not hang in there, jaw to jaw, against Oklahoma. "I believe our players actually think they can. A lot of our players don't give a flip for Oklahoma . . . Texas has to develop a football tradition. It had it once but lost it. When we get one, maybe we can stop that bloodletting up at Dallas and turn it into a good show."

Texas students could feel something special might happen when they arrived in Dallas. A UT student, Darrell Jordan, president of UT's freshman class (and a future president of the Texas Bar Association) and member of the Longhorns' Cowboys spirit group that shot the cannon and tended to Bevo the Steer at the games, remembers riding from Austin to Dallas in the Sigma Chi's charter bus, a ride of about three hours.

"Every Sigma Chi on the bus, and his date, was given a fifth of whiskey," remembers Jordan. "And they had a contest to see which couple would be the first to finish their bottle. The prize was another free bottle. By the time the bus got to Dallas and the Adolphus hotel, where everyone stayed that year, everyone who got off the bus was knee-walking drunk." Highways leading into Dallas from north and south were crammed with busloads of equally afflicted passengers.

At the proud Adolphus, the staff was prepared. Or thought

Refugees from the Oklahoma Dust Bowl arrive in California seeking a new life. The grim aftertaste of hard times was washed away by a fierce state pride engendered by great Sooners football teams—and beating Texas was the best elixir of all. *(© Corbis)*

ABOVE: When Bobby Layne missed his first practice, he explained his whereabouts: "Coach, you don't even *want* to know." Despite Layne's flair for the night life, the Longhorns' quarterback led his team to four straight wins over Oklahoma in the robust postwar years. *(© Corbis)*

BELOW: Of Bud Wilkinson *(left)*, Bear Bryant said, "Bud always looked like he'd just stepped out of the barbershop. I wish I had his class." Wilkinson, in his prime years as coach of the Oklahoma Sooners, was indeed in a class of his own. Sportswriter Joe Williams and another coaching legend, TCU's Dutch Meyer *(right)*, pay homage to the "smiling master." *(© Corbis)*

Every October, Fair Park in Dallas becomes the culture center of the Flatlands Universe—particularly on the Saturday of the Texas-OU game. This photo from 1955 shows the stands in the Cotton Bowl filling with fans before game time while more swarm the Midway. Through the years this has become a recurring scenario of color, excitement, and high-voltage anticipation. *(Courtesy of the State Fair of Texas)*

The Oklahoma football teams of the 1950s were celebrated as the Cadillacs of the Prairies. Bud Wilkinson, pictured with perhaps his greatest team in 1956, crafted a precision unit that won a record forty-seven straight games. *(© Corbis)*

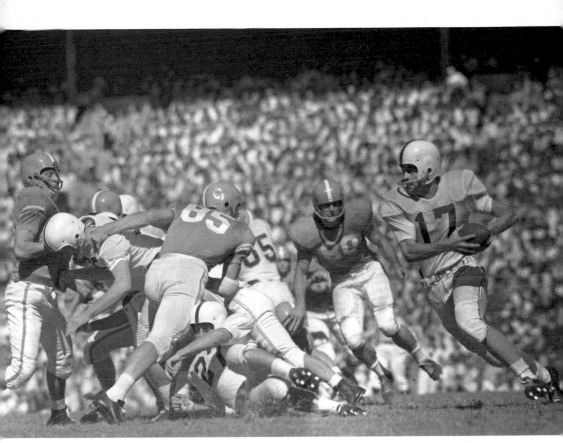

According to the celebrated show tune, Oklahoma is where "the wind comes sweeping down the plains." The Oklahoma Sooners of the Bud Wilkinson era exemplified that. Jimmy Harris directs the swift and relentless Oklahoma offense against Texas in 1955. *(Courtesy of the Dallas Public Library)*

Elated Oklahomans storm the field in 1950 after the Sooners beat Texas, 14–13, splintering the wooden goal posts for souvenirs of the occasion. The crowd scene for the annual Texas-OU game displays the enduring history of sometimes out-of-control behavior by fans of both teams, and for years the Dallas jail was as overbooked as the local hotels. *(Courtesy of the Dallas Public Library)*

Though he stood barely five feet tall (if that), UT trainer Frank Medina was feared by players seemingly twice his size because of his relentless conditioning and rehab program, which remains legendary in Austin. *(Courtesy of the University of Texas Sports Photography Department)*

UT linebacker Tommy Nobis, with his nineteen-inch neck, fortified the Texas defense in the glory years of the 1960s. Oklahoma managed only two touchdowns in three games (1963–65) against Nobis and his orange-clad ilk.
(© Corbis)

Darrell Royal conducts practice—although UT practice uniforms were almost identical to its no-frills look on autumn Saturdays. "These are work clothes," Royal explained. When the Longhorns ran onto the field, fans weren't sure whether they were there to play a football game or to paint the stadium.
(© Corbis)

In the much-hyped 1963 game that featured the top-ranked Sooners against the second-ranked Longhorns, Phil Harris follows fullback Harold Philipp to score a touchdown that gave the Longhorns an insurmountable lead. Texas won 28–7, and proceeded from there to the national championship. (*Courtesy of the University of Texas Sports Photography Department*)

Invented by a UT cheerleader in the mid-fifties, the Longhorns' Hook 'Em Horns salute, as demonstrated by retro-clad Longhorns at the 1963 Oklahoma game, ignites deep resentment among Sooners loyalists. They hate it, in fact, and respond with a derisive, inverted version of the Hook 'Em sign. *(Courtesy of the Dallas Public Library)*

For several decades Native American culture in Oklahoma was synonymous with the warrior spirit of the Sooners football team. Little Red, the unofficial OU mascot, cheers his team before the 1967 Texas game. The dictates of political correctness took Little Red off the field for good in the early 1970s. *(Courtesy of the Dallas Public Library)*

it was. Like the teams on the field, the hotel people needed to be primed and ready. "Ordinarily the weekend required only fifteen extra security guards to patrol the halls and break up the usual good-natured fights," recalls Randall Davis, who bore the task of managing the Adolphus in those perilous years of the 1950s. Sometimes those fights were so good-natured, somebody occasionally would get his good-natured teeth knocked out, and the hotel would also employ an extra doctor to remain on call throughout the weekend. So everything would be under control. But then came what the Adolphus people called "*that* year"— 1958.

The state of Texas, historically, has been the scene of some damn fine explosions, such as the firecracker factory in Fort Worth in the mid-1950s and the Monsanto chemical plant blowup in Texas City in 1947. Rattled windows all the way to Denver. Yet for sheer seismic impact, even that might have been eclipsed by the blast that occurred in Dallas after Texas finally beat Oklahoma.

Here's a bare-bones summary of what took place. Playing under heavy, dark clouds, the Longhorns scored the first touchdown, then went and made a two-point conversion. That year, '58, was the year that the two-point alternative had come into effect, and coaches didn't know what to make of it. Obviously the point was to help cut down on the number of tie games. Nobody liked those. A tie, as they say in Arkansas, is like sleeping with your sister. Darrell Royal didn't care for the two-point business because he felt it would put more pressure on the coaches, and from his perspective, the sideline game-day experience was stressful enough already.

Royal knew too that drastic measures had to be employed to beat Oklahoma and stop the Sooners' six-year tyranny in the Dallas series. So the play was a straight dive with Don Allen running behind left guard H. G. Anderson. "We decided before the game that if we scored first, we would go for two," Royal said. "When we lined up, they had to be expecting us to run some floozie-doozie play. It was just a plain old handoff, but simple as it was, we'd worked on it and worked on it. The players had so much confidence that it would work, and it did. H.G. [the lead blocker] just stuck his hat in the Oklahoma player's stomach so that only the ear flaps were showing."

The Sooners stormed back in the second half, just like Royal knew they would, and took the lead on something of a fluke. Someone dislodged the football from Texas fullback Mike Dowdle, and Oklahoma guard Jim David retrieved it before he hit the field and chugged twenty-four yards for the go-ahead touchdown.

The Longhorns scored late, completing a fourth-quarter march punctuated by several of those forward passes that Royal so distrusted. From the seven-yard line, Bobby Lackey threw a jump pass to end Bob Bryant, who was uncovered in the end zone. While another quarterback, Vince Matthews, had directed most of the winning drive, Royal sent Lackey in for the express purpose of throwing the jump. "He's a big lanky kid, and I wanted someone tall enough to see over the Oklahoma linemen."

"We tried the same play against Tulane, but I had to ground it because our ends couldn't get past the line of scrimmage," Lackey remarked. Lackey, who commented when Royal was hired that he looked not much older than most of the players, kicked the extra point that provided UT its 15–14 edge, then made a one-handed stab (this still in the era when college players competed on both sides of the ball) to end a furious OU comeback bid. One sportswriter, Blackie Sherrod of the *Dallas Times-Herald*, felt it might have been best that OU didn't seal a miracle finish. "This, truly, would have been too much," he wrote. "The sagging inhabitants of the big concrete walls couldn't have stood much more. The crowded populace of 76,000 would have turned to stone and remained there for years to come, studied by scientists, stared at by tourists, and climbed over by small boys on the way to school."

As it was, the gun finally sounded and, according to the UT newspaper, "Smokey the cannon boomed the news of the great victory." The Texas supporters in the Cotton Bowl went stark raving nuts. It was also reported that "swarms of students raced to the end zone and reduced the goal posts to splinters." One Oklahoma fan went down there, too, and was knocked unconscious. UT players danced in circles. Texas's 15–14 win over Arkansas in the 1969 big shootout—or Game of the Century or Richard Nixon Bowl, et cetera—is remembered as the biggest achievement of Royal's career. Royal, though, might have seen that this other 15–14 win, his first against the Sooners, would be the one he most cherished. (The coach chose to go for the two-point conversion try after the Horns' *first* TD in the Arkansas game, too.)

After the '58 OU game, two old coaches sat in the press-box and marveled at what they had witnessed. Blair Cherry, the most recent UT coach to have won against the Sooners and who had been forced out of the office after he couldn't do it again, talked about Royal. "He is smart. Very smart. That young man is a good leader, a gentleman, and a fine coach. And didn't those kids look poised and great today?"

Homer Norton, a onetime blood foe of the Longhorns' cause when he coached at Texas A&M and the last successful coach at Aggieland until Bear Bryant arrived, said, "The game today was an example, a perfect example, of both teams, and particularly Texas, playing from the heart. The fans saw every defense in the book and every offense they'd read about for the last three years. Split-T, the T, single wing, unbalanced line, split line, spread, and spread flanker. Everything you wanted to see in a football game was out there today." And since Kern Tips was broadcasting the game for Humble Oil, you can bet that both teams ran the old dipsy-doodle at some point as well.

Amid the ritual madness on the Cotton Bowl floor, Royal met his mentor, Wilkinson, at midfield. "You beat us bad," Bud told him, and before Royal could respond, two UT players hoisted their coach on their shoulders and carried him to the tunnel leading to the locker room. "We quit, and they didn't," said OU's Steve Jennings.

UT fans in the Cotton Bowl didn't quit when the game was over, either. They returned to downtown Dallas and trashed everything in sight. Jane Peterson, whose older sister Ann was Sweetheart of the University of Texas, was a UT freshman in 1958. "It was my first year, and I expected it to be rowdy, just from what I had heard. But it was total chaos! Windows were broken out of buildings all along St. Paul and Akard streets, and from hotel windows, airborne furniture landed on the sidewalk of Commerce."

Measures were employed so that future Texas-OU weekends might become, as the manager of the Adolphus put it, "a lesser nightmare." Those measures would be futile, and for the Oklahoma Sooners, the nightmare on the football field would continue for another eight years.

5

Full Moon over Norman

If those Oklahoma fans were prone to rent the whole top floor of the best hotels in town on football weekends, they had picked up the habit from Bud Wilkinson's Sooners. Bud moved them into the penthouse of NCAA football—the Presidential Suite right at the top of AP and UPI polls. From there, Oklahoma stared down on the Tennessees and Notre Dames and Michigan States, and the view was breathtaking. Hell. The Sooners could see across the river, where the Texas Longhorns and their fans knew all too well that the only thing that might go right on OU weekend was the Friday-night debauchery. By 1955, while the Sooners were scorching the landscape with a forty-seven-game winning streak that seemed like it might outlive the Eisenhower administration, the Longhorns were being hammered from one end of the state to the other by the likes of the Rice Owls and the TCU Horned Frogs. The Texas fans could find some consolation from the fact that while UT was struggling to stay on the field with the Sooners, nobody else was doing it, either. What did they call the Big Eight Conference at first? Oklahoma and the Seven Dwarfs.

If it was the influx of Texas-bred football talent that contributed so significantly to the force that impelled Bud Wilkinson's Sooners to the NCAA mountaintop, the arrival of two Texans in the Norman arsenal might have been the motivating factors that guided the brilliant coach's decision to seek to sample the lifestyle of a United States senator. Joe Don Looney's herculean gridiron talents came with off-the-playing-field behavioral extremes that almost guaranteed that any person responsible for coaching such a beast would eventually contract a stomach ulcer the size of an Osage orange.

On Joe Don Looney's behalf, it could be argued that Wilkinson almost certainly realized what he was getting into when he recruited such a liberated spirit. Before the arrival of Looney, Wilkinson had sampled a sneak preview of the mind-set in the person of the incomparable Edward "Wahoo" McDaniel. With a distinguished Native American lineage, Wahoo, who was actually Wahoo McDaniel Jr., had been a do-it-all practitioner of all things athletic—the second coming of Jim Thorpe himself, some would argue. So, as a teenager, McDaniel had already achieved folk-legend status in Midland, situated in the heart of the great American postwar petroplex.

Wahoo had starred as a Pony League baseball player on a team that won a state championship and was coached by a man who would become the forty-first president of the United States, George Herbert Walker Bush. Like everyone else who would experience Wahoo firsthand, if even for a day, President Bush would remember McDaniel for the rest of his life. McDaniel's high school baseball coach benched Wahoo for skipping baseball practice to work out with the track team. Wahoo got into the game late, socked the winning home run, trotted around the bases, shot the coach the finger as he crossed home plate, kept on running, and never put on a baseball uniform again.

Nobody in Midland cared a lick about Wahoo's status in

the diamond. Friday night in the fall was what those folks, then and now, deem as all that matters. Wahoo was a single wing for coach Ralph "Tugboat" Jones and the Midland Bulldogs. In this top-of-the-marquee role, McDaniel was not a man among children but a man among some hard-ass teenagers, and that was good enough for him. Wilkinson's recruiting staff had circled Wahoo as a top-priority recruit. Perhaps they might have thought otherwise had they known that Wahoo would stand in the huddle early in games and estimate the crowd, and if the people in the grandstands numbered fewer than 8,000, he would announce to his teammates that "if these people don't care enough to come and watch Wahoo, then nobody's gonna see the real Wahoo tonight." Tugboat Jones might have anguished when Wahoo would take the evening off, effort-wise, but there wasn't a hell of a lot he could do about it. McDaniel, equipped with the hindquarters of a grizzly bear, was born to run. That much was substantiated once and for all in McDaniel's last high school game against Midland's blood rival, the Odessa Broncos.

The Midland-Odessa rivalry was perhaps as blood-intense as any in Texas high school football. Separated by twenty miles of moonscape across the flattest, driest, most godforsaken terrain this side of the Gobi Desert, the communities were anything but sister cities. Odessa was regarded as the home base to men who manned the derricks, the roughnecks, the roustabouts and tool pushers. Theirs was a hazardous occupation. Working the rigs was one of the best and quickest ways possible to lose a finger. Midland, so-called because it's halfway between Fort Worth and El Paso, served as headquarters for the people who pulled the financial levers for the region. They had a saying in the area: Midland will break your spirit, Odessa will break your jaw. So it had been the jaw-busters who had been ruling the gridiron series in the mid-1950s. The Bulldogs had won the previous ten installments of the series, which was traditionally played as a regular season finale on Thanksgiving afternoon.

In 1955, Ted Battle, sportswriter for the Midland newspaper, produced a story predicting that Odessa, the hated foe, would shortly be running the streak to eleven straight. The ink had scarcely dried on the newsprint when Battle picked up his telephone at the office. The Midland Bulldogs tailback, Wahoo McDaniel, was on the other end of the line. "Wahoo essentially told me I was full of crap, and he called me out," Battle would remember.

"He bet me a thousand dollars that Midland was going to win." Since a thousand dollars constituted about two and a half months' salary, Battle demurred. Which was wise. McDaniel ran for more than 250 yards, scored four touchdowns, and Odessa's winning streak was over. With the Oklahoma Sooners midstride in that cherished forty-seven-game victory surge that defines the OU program to this day, Wahoo and the Bud Wilkinson football machine seemed a natural partnership. Playing for Oklahoma, Wahoo, at least, wouldn't need to count the empty seats in the grandstand to decide whether or not to bring his A-game. As fullback, Wahoo had Heisman Trophy written all over him. But in the process of being groomed as the Sooners' latest running star, a funny thing happened. OU recruited Prentice Gautt, its first-ever African-American player. Racial enlightenment being what it was in that time and place, the arrival of Gautt into the program might have created some, shall we say, unrest among certain aspects of the Sooners fan base. But with Bud Wilkinson summoning the fullback into the OU football family, the appearance of the first black on the Sooner team was—if not universally applauded—at least greeted with acceptance by the Oklahoma grid-community.

Just one catch, as far as Wahoo McDaniel was concerned.

Since Wilkinson had made the dramatic move to initiate Gautt into the program, Gautt was damn sure going to play. Prior to McDaniel's sophomore season, the coaching staff approached Wahoo with an interesting proposition: Why not switch to end? McDaniel readily complied. The move worked well for all parties involved. However, because Wahoo would never have the opportunity to run with the football, his name wouldn't be associated with the on-the-field greats of Sooner folklore. So Wahoo turned to off-the-field exploits to seal his legendary rank in Norman.

McDaniel, who was not averse to offering outlandish betting propositions, as that Midland sportswriter had learned, concocted a humdinger during an idle off-season hour in the OU football dorm. Wahoo wagered a couple of teammates that he could, at that very moment, take off running from the front door of the dorm and make it to the Oklahoma City city limits within six hours. The distance was just more than forty miles. He was wearing shorts and a pair of flimsy sneakers that were popular at the time. Cross-countries, they called them, but the shoes were hardly ideal for distance running. Wahoo didn't care. As McDaniel loped toward the state capital, word of his exploit spread around the campus, and soon a caravan of cars was following the runner along the highway. A radio station mobile unit would join the chase, broadcasting live. McDaniel won the bet, and with it, a strange kind of notoriety.

Soon McDaniel was answering challenges from OU fraternities offering to organize relay teams to compete against him in long-distance excursions. Wahoo beat the frat boys every time. "I damn near got beat this one time—had to sprint to catch a guy at the finish—but that was the only time it was close," McDaniel told me in 2001 when I interviewed him for a "where are they now" piece for *Sports Illustrated.*

"Bud heard about that stuff, of course, and he didn't like it. I mean, pulling stunts wasn't something that he really condoned among his players, but I didn't want to quit, because, well, it was a good fund-raising effort for old Wahoo."

Perhaps those long-distance running exhibitions were not the primary source of Bud Wilkinson's concern. Undoubtedly, Wilkinson had also learned of Wahoo's willing response to a dare that involved drinking motor oil. "I didn't chugalug the whole quart, contrary to the rumor. Only had a few spoonfuls, actually," he would tell me.

What's your favorite highball? Quaker State 30 weight?

"Actually, I'd have to say Sinclair 10W-40," McDaniel responded, showing no regrets. "For days afterward, in practice, I could feel the stuff oozing out of my pores. I smelled like an old tractor." From this, Wilkinson might have properly concluded that in Wahoo, he had a football player who might someday accidentally shoot his tag-team partner in the leg while pistol-whipping a disgruntled fan who attacked him after a pro-wrestling event in Atlanta.

As an Oklahoma Sooner, McDaniel would participate in the only victorious effort in the Texas game, and that was as a sophomore in 1957—about a month before the Sooners' amazing forty-seven-game streak that would end in the 7–0 loss to Notre Dame. The next year, Wahoo and OU would lose to the Steers, and by the time McDaniel's eligibility ended at Norman, the Bud Wilkinson football dynasty was coming to its end. In McDaniel's final game in an Oklahoma uniform, the Sooners traveled to Lincoln and lost to the Nebraska Cornhuskers—OU's first conference loss in thirteen years. Wahoo's legacy to the Oklahoma program, a tribute to what one might call his "Jim Thorpe athleticism," was that for forty years, McDaniel held the record for the longest punt in OU history. Ninety-four yards.

Wilkinson realized then that those lyrical Oklahoma winds that came sweeping down the plains were the winds of change. In Wahoo McDaniel, Bud detected the first traces of the new American college athlete. The final vestiges of what is known as the Greatest Generation—the one that won World War II and went to school on the GI Bill, the "yes sir–no sir" crew-cut and flattop boys who would never muster the temerity to question (much less challenge) authority or the proper chain of command— were gradually giving way to a different kind of football player. The Free Spirit. The child of the sixties. In such a character as Wahoo, who was clearly marching to the beat of his own tom-tom, Bud could detect that a different mood among younger Americans, more loose, more reckless, was gathering along the next horizon.

McDaniel was dying of kidney disease when I interviewed him in North Carolina. He needed a transplant and hoped to last long enough to raise his teenage son, Zach, to self-sufficiency. Wahoo didn't make it, and at a memorial service Zach eulogized Wahoo as "the only father I ever heard of who'd let his son shoot a rifle inside the house." Wahoo was a helluva guy, and an incredibly versatile football player. The fullback who agreed to play end would actually start at offensive guard for the Houston Oilers when they defeated the (then) Los Angeles Chargers in the first-ever championship game of the American Football League. Later, he gained the adoration of New York Jets fans playing yet another position—linebacker.

McDaniel abandoned football for the more lucrative ranks of pro wrestling, where he won a generation of admirers for his participation in Indian strap matches and similar competitions that remain unsanctioned by the International Olympic Committee. Wahoo, who was married five times, obviously undertook an unconventional approach to his day-to-day affairs. The last thing Wahoo told me, however, was that he looked back on his

OU days as the most fulfilling ones of his life, and he applauded the efforts of coach Bob Stoops, whose teams were kicking UT silly. "Yeah, and sometimes I get requests to do something for my old high school, too. The Midland Bulldogs. But they really haven't won a damn thing since I left, and until they do, then to hell with 'em."

About the same time Wahoo McDaniel was arriving at the Norman campus, circa mid-1950s, a Pony League baseball umpire in Fort Worth called a third strike. Furious, the Pony Leaguer heaved his bat, which landed in the small grandstand and bonked a woman spectator on the head.

"You're outta here!" screamed the ump at the offending player.

"Out of the league?" the player asked.

"No. Just out of the game," the ump told Joe Don Looney.

Thus began a pattern of ejection that would remain with Looney, one of the most memorable personalities in the history of the Texas-Oklahoma football series, for the remainder of his life.

Looney was an only child. His father, Don, had been a star end at TCU and played on the Horned Frogs' national championship team in 1938, one that had been quarterbacked by a Heisman Trophy winner, Davey O'Brien. So Don Looney was an icon in Fort Worth, and Joe Don felt that he needed to establish an identity of his own. At McLean Junior High, Joe Don went and got himself elected cheerleader. Looney, though, realized that he was genetically endowed with some rare athletic gifts. By the time Joe Don reached high school, he couldn't help himself any longer. As a junior at Paschal High, he ran track and sprinted stride for stride with Carter Riverside's Bill Kemp down the straightaway at Farrington Field in the 440-yard relay finals in the district championship meet, and cut a four-yard deficit to about a yard and a half at the finish line. That was significant for a couple of reasons: Bill Kemp went on to become a trivia answer—he won the 100-yard dash at the Drake Relays in 1961, which was the first event ever televised on *ABC's Wide World of Sports*. And Looney, when he was making up ground back at the high school, was already about twice the size of Bill Kemp.

Looney played varsity football at Paschal with mixed results. His thirty-yard touchdown run against hated rival Arlington Heights won the game for Paschal, but Joe Don would also leave the field on a stretcher, knocked cold as a wedge. (Actually, the most famous person on the field that night was the Arlington Heights homecoming queen, Gunilla Hutton, who went on to be Nurse Goodbody on *Hee Haw*.)

College coaches were fascinated by the potential of Looney's unquestionable physical skills. But as Darrell Royal himself used to like to say: Potential means you ain't done it yet. Also, the college coaches had already become skeptical of Joe Don's commitment to the notion of team concept. They had reason to be, after hearing some stories from Looney's high school coaches at Paschal. For instance, in Looney's senior year, he informed the track coach that he was bowing out of the finals in the 220 at the regional track meet at Ownby Stadium at the SMU campus in Dallas.

The coach was flabbergasted. "What's wrong? Did you pull a hamstring or something?"

"Nah," Looney answered. "I'm just depressed."

Looney told me later that in reality, before finals, he'd enjoyed a heavy pasta lunch at Campisi's restaurant on Mockingbird Lane near the stadium, the same place where American League umpire Steve Palermo would get shot on the front sidewalk. He had dined with a competing runner, Highland Park's John Roderick. "We had a couple of beers at lunch, and afterward,

Roderick showed me his .45 automatic that he kept in his glove compartment. The whole business kind of blew my mind, and I just couldn't really get into running that 220 after that." (Here's a little knee-slapper from the realm of ironic trivia. The winner of the regional 220 race that Saturday, Bill Hill from Garland High, became the district attorney of Dallas County.)

At this juncture of his career, Looney decided that if there was a future for him in the world of the perspiring arts, it would be in track, although he was fostering distant dreams of also perhaps becoming the heavyweight boxing champion of the world. The notion of becoming one of the most celebrated participants in the annals of the Texas-OU grid classic in the Cotton Bowl was the furthest thing from Looney's mind. The summer after finishing high school, Looney drove his '59 Chevy Impala to California, where he obtained a job picking apricots. His purpose was to attend the track meets that led up to the trials for the 1960 Summer Olympic games held in Rome. Looney wanted to mingle with some world-class athletes and study their training techniques. In this, he was somewhat successful. "I had dinner with Dave Davis, a shot-putter, one night," Looney related, describing the most meaningful episode of his Golden State adventures. "Davis ordered a pitcher of beer, took the thing in one hand, and downed it in a couple of swallows. That was impressive, and from then on, I wanted to be just like Dave Davis."

Looney left California and enrolled as a freshman at the University of Texas in September. The track coach at UT, Clyde Littlefield, something of an immortal figure himself, knew that Looney was in school, and some arrangement had been made for Joe Don to practice with the team as a walk-on. Joe Don participated in one practice. "Afterward, Littlefield told me I was one of the best athletes he'd ever seen step on the track at Memorial Stadium. I don't believe he actually meant that, though. Impressed me as being kind of phony." That was the world according to Joe Don Looney in 1960. He never attended another track practice and joined another team—the intramural football B-team for the Kappa Sigma fraternity that Looney pledged after arriving at UT.

Looney and that frat chapter seemed like an excellent fit, at first. The Kappa Sig house was conspicuously situated at the end of the esplanade that runs south of the UT tower, standing equidistant from that landmark and the Texas state capitol building. And the house, for decades, had been occupied by some fairly conspicuous individuals. People such as Buford Jester, the governor of Texas in the late 1940s; Cyrus Rowlett Smith, the founder of American Airlines; Denton Cooley, the world-acclaimed heart surgeon; and Amon Carter Jr., a media magnate and son of the man for whom every public building in Fort Worth was named, including the TCU football stadium that literally cast a tall shadow across the house where Looney had grown up in Fort Worth.

When Looney joined the frat, the group was assembling a group of extremists. In other words, to merit membership in the UT Kappa Sigs, a person had to be extremely rich, or extremely smart, or extremely funny, or extremely socially excessive. Extremely *something,* in other words. It didn't matter what, as long as it was extreme. Naturally Looney was a wonderful fit. At first.

One of Joe Don's early campus companions was another UT pledge from Fort Worth, Craig Metz, whose father, Dick Metz, was the club pro at the Shady Oaks Country Club. The elder Metz had been in the running for the U.S. Open championship one year, but his hopes had been shattered when wrestler George Zaharias, while greeting him with a handshake before the final round, broke a small bone in the golfer's hand. Craig Metz had come to Texas to try out for the baseball team, but like his pal Joe Don never really pursued varsity athletics at UT. He became immersed in the temptations of Austin nightlife, which spilled over into daylife, if one did it right. Metz was paired with Lynda Bird Johnson on a blind date. At the conclusion of the evening, Lynda Bird asked Metz if she could have a bottle of the beer he'd been swilling. She said she sometimes washed her hair in it, at which point Metz belched on the side of Lynda Bird's head and said, "Then how about some spray net?" Dashing and daring, Metz further popularized himself by carving the Greek Kappa Sig letters with a church key into a coffee table in the foyer of Mrs. Ledwidge's high-rent boardinghouse for girls.

Craig Metz, who would eventually take up golf like his father and promptly become one of the best competitive amateurs in the United States, left school at Thanksgiving. He amassed huge losses playing cards in the games that went on virtually around the clock in the basement of the Kappa Sig house and was hanging hot paper all over Austin. Meanwhile, Looney had become the architect of his own reputation. It was a reputation spreading widely across the campus, and it was not a particularly desirable one, even by Kappa Sig standards. A typical Joe Don evening would, in his own words, go like this: "Hey, I'm really getting strong! I walked the check at El Patio [restaurant]. The waiter chased me out into the parking lot, and I punted that son of a bitch about forty-eight yards, clear across the street, against the wind, with about a five-second hang time."

The problem with that story was that it was all too true. Looney always told the truth. His versions of the events that motivated him to such exhibitions of mayhem were always suspect, but nobody would dispute Looney's version of the event itself. Socializing with Looney presented risks. I was with Looney and a few others the night he drove down to San Antonio to attend the world premiere of John Wayne's *The Alamo*. Afterward, leaving the theater and clearly moved by the on-screen experience, Looney declared, in a voice loud enough to be heard across half of San Antonio, "If I outnumbered Davy Crockett fifty to one, I could have killed him, too. Goddamn, fuckin', chickenshit Mexicans . . ."

According to Austin folklore, Looney got kicked out of his UT fraternity after he threw a guy through the big plate-glass window at the Toddle House diner a block from the Kappa Sig house. Like so many stories about Looney, it never happened. Looney's frat pal Craig Metz was the one involved in the Toddle House riot, and he was not the person who did the throwing, but was rather the throw-ee. Looney was dismissed all right, blackballed or "boomed" as the Kappa Sigs called it, but probably on grounds of general principles. His ousting was endorsed by the law office of the Kappa Sig patriarch Frank Erwin, probably the most significant power broker in the UT politics of his era. They waited until the Kappa Sig B-team got upset by the Delts or somebody in the intramural playoffs before giving Joe Don the heave-ho.

He didn't seem to care. Looney knew he wouldn't be in Austin too long, anyway. A test paper he'd brought home from math showed a score of eighteen, and the prof had written across the top, "Mr. Looney—are you joking?"

One important thing did occur in Looney's one-semester UT experience. He decided that he might be interested in playing some football after all. That happened in the stands at the Cotton Bowl at, yes, the Texas-OU game in 1960. The Longhorns dominated the football game from the start. (This would be a down year for the Sooners.) Very down, as Wilkinson's team would finish the season at 3-6-1. OU was trailing Texas late, 17–0, but driving. Sooner fans were screaming, and then UT linebacker Pat Culpepper intercepted a Sooners pass and returned it seventy-eight yards to make the final score 24–0. Longhorns fans went nuts, and Looney, seated in the UT section, announced in that same loud voice that he'd employed at the movies in San Antonio, "Know what? I could get out there and play for Texas right now. Those guys are just a bunch of pussies." A fan in the row in front of Joe Don turned to him and said, "Then why don't you get out there on the field and show us?" Looney, rather than bashing the guy, was already pondering the suggestion. He knew that he wanted to play somewhere—just not at the University of Texas.

He sat in the stands the next week in Austin, where Arkansas upset the Longhorns, 24–23, and rooted for the Hogs. "Texas is a dirty team," Looney decided afterward. "This Texas guy kicked Joe Paul Alberti [the Hogs fullback] right in the nuts. Nobody else saw it but me, I guess. Didn't slow Alberti down—he's tougher than anybody Texas had on the field." So, to Joe Paul Alberti, wherever he is, let it be known for the first time that Joe Paul was Joe Don Looney's first and only football role model.

Joe Don Looney flunked out of Texas in January, moved back to Fort Worth, and enrolled at TCU with the intention of trying out for coach Abe Martin and the Horned Frogs. He abandoned those plans almost at once after learning that he would have to sit out a year before becoming eligible. He lived in the basement of his folks' house that abutted the parking lot at Amon Carter Stadium and pumped iron all day long. Looney would also strap two sets of leg weights known as Elmer's Handicaps onto his ankle and climb up the almost vertical surface of the dam at Benbrook Lake west of town. Often Looney climbed over the fence at the TCU stadium, ran the steps alone, hour after hour, and then went out onto the field and punted a football, high and forty yards downfield, before sprinting down to catch the thing himself.

Throughout his football career, Looney was accused, in the media and in the minds of the sporting public that didn't know better, of squandering his immense sporting talents. He was a natural, all right. Looney could do double backflips on a trampoline like, say, Mary Lou Retton. He could dance like Gene Kelly and drive a golf ball like John Daly. He could truly do anything he damn well wanted to, a jock of all trades, but his critics never realized how passionately and relentlessly Looney had toiled in order to fashion himself into the machine that he was to become.

Nighttime was different, though, and Looney, even in his teens, felt completely at home and at ease in the garish glare of the Fort Worth neon. Cowtown was honky-tonk heaven, and Looney relished the setting. He could not stand the country music on the jukebox (one could not enter a Fort Worth saloon without hearing Floyd Cramer plink-plinking "Last Date" on the piano), but he was tolerant of any setting as long as the beer was cold and in ample supply. I was home from UT at midsemester break and got busted with Looney for drinking underage at a dive in West Vickery next to the Texas & Pacific Railroad yards where we all used to go shoot rats with .22s during our happy days as lads. They called the tavern The Pub. It was a brakeman's bar, and we were popped by a mean man who represented the Texas Liquor Control.

Joe Don was back in there the very next night. "The only time I ever met Looney was in The Pub," recalls a man named Joe Longley, now an Austin lawyer. "I was wearing a white Izod golf shirt, the ones with the little alligators on them. Evidently he didn't like Izod, so he picked up this plastic toothpick off the bar and flicked it at me, and, I'll swear to God, the thing stuck in the shirt like a miniature javelin, and a little bead of blood appeared next to the alligator. He threw his head back, laughed, and said, '*That*'s the way Joe Don Looney does it.' "

I got to see another way that Joe Don "did it" in Fort Worth around New Year's. Now, Looney was wearing a tux at a party that was thrown by the daughter of an eye surgeon, near the Rivercrest Country Club, playpen for the upper crust. An attendee at the soiree was Sid Bass, home on holiday from Yale. Sid had something of a good thing going for him. He was one of the richest little bastards in the world. I knew Sid, having sat next to him in Spanish class in junior high school before his family had shipped him off to prep school at Andover. Late in the evening, Sid Bass attempted to toss a piece of peppermint candy to another guest. He missed, and the candy hit Joe Don in that tree trunk of a neck that he had.

Looney's blood alcohol level was in the danger zone. He told Sid "to cut that shit out." He didn't know who Sid Bass was, and Sid, being a person who could buy downtown Houston with his pocket change and was certainly unused to being addressed in such a manner, reached into the candy jar and flipped another piece in Joe Don's direction. I knew what was coming next and actually stepped over a coffee table in time to intercept Looney and stave off the assault. "For Chrissake! Don't kill Sid!" I spun Looney around and directed him back toward the kitchen, where the booze was being poured. Later, a shaken Sid Bass offered me thanks.

I include this happening only because that was my only meaningful contribution to the Texas-Oklahoma football series. Had Looney socked Sid Bass, he might not have actually killed him, but certainly would have inflicted life-threatening cranial damage. Had that occurred, the Bass family would have seen to it that Looney was sent away for about eighty years, and Bud Wilkinson would have been deprived of the opportunity to meet the most frustrating football player he would ever coach.

Looney—though it was hardly his intention—was gathering a citywide reputation as the most notorious saloon patron to hit Fort Worth since Doc Holliday. Perhaps the most notable of frequent Mount Looney eruptions took place in the parking lot of the 19th Hole, a dive on University Drive popular with TCU kids. Looney duked it out with a Horned Frogs basketball player, David Warnell. His teammate, six-foot-nine Stan Farr, who would be shot to death in the most celebrated murder case in Fort Worth history, was in the audience and watched Looney punch out Warnell. Joe Don's first-round TKO earned him persona non grata status on the TCU campus and in parts of the surrounding neighborhood.

Looney played golf at the Worth Hills muni course that abuts the college—the same course immortalized as Goat Hills in various Dan Jenkins–authored projects. He stood admiring the flight of his tee shot on a Par 4 hold that ran along Stadium Drive—damn near drove the green—and watched as a little kid ran out of a house across the street, picked up Looney's golf ball, then ran back inside. A guy in the threesome fell over laughing and said, "That's a two-stroke penalty, Joe Don." Looney sprinted down the fairway, carrying his driver in his right hand, and ran across the street, the spikes on his golf shoes making a *klat-klat-klat* noise on the pavement. He pounded on the front door, and from within, a woman's voice commanded, "You get away from here before I call the police."

The Looney situation was that he was seeking a higher plane—cosmically, that is—and Fort Worth could be a frustrating place to try to accomplish that. His journey to awareness began after he read Hermann Hesse's *Siddhartha*. Looney identified with the young prince. "Siddhartha—the strong, the beautiful, moving with his lithe-limbed walk . . . love stirred in the hearts of the young daughters of the brahmins when Siddhartha walked through the city streets with his radiant brow, his imperial grace, with his slender hips." Looney read that and said, "Yep, that's me, all right."

Of course, in the case of his literary model, it was, "Yes, everyone loved Siddhartha. He aroused joy in everyone, he was a delight to all." Well, that's where the Siddhartha–Joe Don Looney connection really jumps the track. Most people felt that it was only a matter of time before Joe Don got himself shot. If Joe Don had any competition for the rank of Fort Worth's premier ass kicker, it would have been Rudy Mauser, a former center on the Kansas Jayhawks football team. "So who do you think is the baddest of the bad, you or Rudy?" The question was posed to Looney, and he sighed, "I guess there's just one way to find out.

"Send Rudy over to beat the crap out of David Warnell, and then Warnell can tell us." Most everything Looney did, even at age eighteen, he accomplished with a rare kind of panache.

The challenge Looney then encountered was that he was primed and poised to conquer the kingdom of American athletics, but he lacked the proper stage setting to exploit his talents or from which to expand his arena from the barroom parking lot. Up to this point, Looney's best playing surface was asphalt. His one attempt at boxing produced a jagged outcome. An experienced Golden Gloves heavyweight was making Looney look awkward in an outdoor ring at Rockwood Park. Finally, in the second round, Looney landed a punch. His opponent promptly swallowed his tongue and went into convulsions. Afterward, the man in charge of the event approached Looney and told him, "You damn near killed that boy! Don't ever come back here again!" Thus ended Looney's ring career. Football loomed as Looney's only immediate alternative, and his father, Don, quietly came to Joe Don's rescue. Don Looney contacted the football coach at Cameron Junior College in Lawton, Oklahoma, just across the Red River from Wichita Falls, and convinced Leroy Montgomery to give Joe Don a dorm room and a shot at the football team.

This would become the first and only win-win situation that Looney ever encountered in his athletic career. The players mostly thought that Looney was a tackle when he arrived for practice and were stunned that a player of his size could run so fast, so explosively. He was accepted immediately. Looney, for his part, felt at home at Cameron. The players referred to the place as "UCLA . . . University of Cameron (Lawton area)," and Looney respected the coach—particularly after what happened the night before a road game. Looney said that Montgomery had driven the team bus into a nearby town for a couple of cold ones, then had run the bus into a ditch on his way back to the motel, where it got stuck. Not the kind of thing that one might expect from, say, Bud Wilkinson.

Cameron's team won all of its regular-season games, with Looney hard, and on some occasions impossible, to stop from his fullback position. The team was invited to play in the Junior College Rose Bowl in Pasadena. A collection of college scouts came to see the game, with Joe Don Looney of particular interest. Looney played his usual game, and afterward was approached with several scholarships from major colleges. If the scouts had really been paying attention, they might have noticed something kind of odd about Joe Don's showing up at Pasadena. Namely, his pants.

A few hours before the kickoff, Looney had informed the Cameron equipment manager that he intended to wear his practice pants in the game itself. The practice pants fit better, were more comfortable, and enabled him to run faster and play better. The problem was that Cameron's practice pants were white, while the game pants were black. Leroy Montgomery settled the issue. They dyed Looney's practice pants black. "They came out kind of half black," Looney said. "I mean, I went ahead and wore the dyed pants in the game, but they looked like hell." That was Joe Don's only lingering recollection of his time at the Junior Rose Bowl game.

Looney led Cameron to victory in Pasadena, bad pants and all, then began to sift through a variety of scholarship offers. Tennessee. Wisconsin. And the Oklahoma Sooners. This was a notable deviation from Bud Wilkinson's policy of not recruiting junior college players. At an earlier time, back in the glorious gold rush days of that forty-seven-straight winning streak, Wilkinson probably would have passed on a prospect like Looney. In his precisely woven team concept, the sudden appearance of a stranger in Wilkinson's backfield might have created some unrest in the ranks—particularly a stranger with Looney's outlaw reputation.

Hard times in Dallas now caused Wilkinson to rethink his non-JUCO policy. The Sooners had lost four straight to Darrell Royal's Longhorns, the new darlings of the great Southwest. That rocket-fueled Sooners offense, the scourge of the prairies, seemed to be running into quicksand in the Dallas series. OU had scored exactly one touchdown against those damn hated Longhorns. Royal had gained the upper hand in the series by putting a defense on the field that could outrun the Sooners offense. Bud needed firepower. So, in those desperate times, Wilkinson needed a quick fix, and the remedy seemed at hand in the intriguing form of Looney. What he did, in actuality, was bring in a mercenary. Bud might just as well have hired

a guy out of the employment ads in *Soldier of Fortune* magazine. That's how many of Looney's new teammates could have
viewed his appearance on the roster in the fall 1962 season. Any
possible side effects on the team from the arrival of a hired gun
vanished very suddenly in Oklahoma's home opener.

The Sooners were trailing Syracuse in the fourth quarter.
Syracuse was coached by Ben Schwartzwalder, the man who
issued the greatest postgame quote in the history of college
sports. It had happened after Syracuse beat Texas in the 1960
Cotton Bowl. That game was an urban rumble alley and some
of the Texas players weren't exactly candidates for the sportsmanship award, which was unusual for a Darrell Royal–coached
team. Afterward, Schwartzwalder was furious with one of the
game officials (he had a right to be, too) and said, "In World
War II, I stuck eight-inch knives into guys I didn't hate as much
as I hate him."

The Syracuse team that opened the year at OU was coming in after a tragic summertime. The previous season, the team
had produced the first black Heisman Trophy winner, Ernie
Davis, who died of leukemia in August. Joe Don Looney had
been a huge fan of Davis and didn't believe it when somebody
said they'd heard that he was dying. "Ernie Davis?" I remember
Looney saying. "Yeah, right. And I've got cancer of the heart."

Ernie Davis died, though, and Looney found himself trotting onto the field with 2:10 to play and the Sooners trailing,
3–0. As the score suggested, Oklahoma's offense had been stag-
nant. Looney entered the Sooners huddle, and the quarterback,
Monte Deere from Amarillo, inquired, in what Looney would
later describe as "that West Texas accent of Monte's," "What'sa
play, Joe Don?"

And Looney said, "Just gimme the ball." So Deere gave
Looney the ball, and he ripped through the entire Syracuse

defense and raced sixty-five yards for a touchdown. Oklahoma won, 7–3. Nobody could remember the last time a Sooners player had made a come-from-behind, fourth-quarter touchdown run like that one. Of course, there had not been that many opportunities, since OU hadn't been behind very much for the previous fifteen years. So Bud Wilkinson and Looney both knew that he was now the headline attraction for the 1962 Oklahoma football team, and neither man could change that, even if he'd wanted to. So the next morning, Looney went to church "just to be seen."

The Wilkinson-Looney partnership was uneasy from the outset. Wilkinson, throughout his coaching tenure at Oklahoma, would preach that if a football team was to be any good, every player must subordinate personal goals for the good of the team. Bud's new backfield blaster remained convinced that anarchy was the more desirable pathway to the stars. "Authority," Looney said, "is simply the ability to screw people."

Every great coach, Wilkinson included, possesses mechanisms that enable him to truly get into the athlete's head, penetrate the mind. So when Bud Wilkinson entered the inner sanctum that was Looney's head, what he saw probably scared the bejesus out of him, and he left at once. Wilkinson would later reflect on Looney: "He was the greatest athlete and craziest sociopath I ever coached."

Notre Dame beat OU in Norman the next game. No Joe Don voodoo this time, not against the Roman Catholic hex. Then Oklahoma was a substantial underdog going into the Texas game.

In Austin, Darrell Royal's team was coping with the raw fact that this 1962 team might not be as potent as the previous year's team. The 1961 Longhorns had been Royal's best to date, featuring the running skills of tailback Jimmy Saxton. As a rural youth, Saxton used to roam the fields, chasing down jackrabbits in his cowboy boots. According to his coach, Saxton was, on various occasions, "quick as a bucket of minnows" and "moving faster than small-town gossip." I know that Darrell Royal attained happiness and joy as the football coach in Austin, but he blew a better career in improv.

Saxton's team made it to number one in the country. Nine games deep into the season, Saxton made the mistake of having his face appear on the cover of *Sports Illustrated*. So a TCU lineman, Bobby Plummer, put a knee on Saxton's helmet, ending his day, and TCU pulled a huge upset in Austin, 6–0. The Frogs scored on a flea-flicker, Sonny Gibbs to Buddy Iles. The next year, speaking to reporters on the Southwest Conference preseason press tour about his desire to attain a degree, Gibbs said, "I want to get that horse hide, or sheep hide, or whatever the fuck they call it."

That was the second time in three years that the Horned Frogs had ruined an unbeaten season for Texas. After the 1961 disappointment, Royal did something he rarely did, which was say something that would come back and bite him on the ass. "TCU is like a cockroach," he said. "It's not what they pick up and carry off that's the problem, it's what they fall into and mess up." That team redeemed itself with a win over some behemoths from Ole Miss in the Cotton Bowl.

Without Saxton, the Texas attack wasn't as mesmerizing as previous editions. The quarterback, John Genung from Wichita Falls, was pretty much a no-trick pony. Texas would win its games on defense in 1962 and was a substantial favorite to beat the Sooners.

The Friday night pregame party in 1962 would be the last I would experience as a collegian. It was typical of any one of hundreds that were taking place around the Dallas–Fort Worth area. This was at some dude ranch, around Grapevine, where the DFW airport is now. Literally twenty kegs of beer were on tap, and eight of them were already floating when the band came on.

They began to sing:

> *A-sshole . . . a-sshole—*
> *A soldier went to war . . .*
> *His piss . . . his piss—*
> *His pistol at his side . . .*
> *My cunt . . . my cunt—*
> *My country 'tis of thee . . .*

I'll stop now because, after that, the song got low-rent.

Outside, on the grounds of the dude ranch, one of the fraternity gentlemen was with his girlfriend and experiencing love and its warm embrace as it can feel only inside an empty stagecoach. They'd been spotted, though, and the eyes of Texas and half the party were upon them, and three of the brothers crept behind the stagecoach, then began to push it, until it careened down a steep hill, bounced into a creek bed, and tumped over.

The Texas-OU weekend is hard on relationships. We cannot stress this point enough. People just get too damn drunk. Those lovebirds in the stagecoach broke up at once. The good news came thirty years later, when the gal had a hysterectomy and they found the guy's senior ring.

Darrell Royal, in his preparations for the '62 OU game, had been worried throughout the week. Now in his fifth season at Texas, he thought that the Sooners offense offered the scariest challenge he'd faced in the Dallas series to date. When the Longhorns came onto the field for pregame warmups, they could not help but notice the Sooners on the other side of the

Cotton Bowl bashing into each other like in a two-a-day practice. Clearly, Oklahoma was primed for a kamikaze effort. In the pregame coin toss, UT captains Pat Culpepper and Perry McWilliams found that the Sooners were so emotionally charged that their OU counterparts were crying when they met at midfield. The football game that took place was satisfying for neither side, really. Neither the players nor the fans.

Texas made a touchdown when McWilliams, a guard, recovered a fumbled pitchout in the OU end zone. And that was all Texas had to offer, thrillwise, the rest of the game.

Oklahoma came up with the only real action late in the first half. Ron Fletcher, a fifth-string quarterback, who played his senior high school season in France and played hardly at all at Oklahoma because you could hide him in a suitcase, entered the game at halfback. He took a pitchout and threw a thirty-five-yard completion to a player who was not even on the OU traveling roster and had come to Dallas on his own. His name was Lance Rentzel.

So Oklahoma ran the same play, to the other side of the field this time, for a touchdown. Rentzel had gotten behind UT defender Jim Hudson, who later would play with the group known as the University of Texas at Broadway when they won Super Bowl III. Of the two-play, Fletcher-to-Rentzel TD shocker, Dallas writer Blackie Sherrod would note that the "Longhorns' pass defense looked as embarrassed as Jackie Kennedy caught in a hock shop." In retrospect, they shouldn't have been embarrassed. Sliding behind secondaries was something that Rentzel was damn good at, as Vince Lombardi and the Packers later discovered in the Ice Bowl game. Rentzel, wearing a short-sleeve jersey while everybody else was bundled up like astronauts walking on the moon, caught that long halfback pass from Dan Reeves—the same play that worked against the Longhorns.

If Rentzel hadn't made that catch in the Ice Bowl, Bart Starr never would have become a hero, because he wouldn't have needed to.

The Sooners' sucker-punch touchdown was timed to provide the team with a terrific psychological energy boost just prior to halftime. What happened next was a testimonial to Royal's every-last-detail attention to special-teams play. In a team meeting the morning of the game, at the Melrose Hotel, Royal distributed "kicking sheets" to the players and pored over every contingency that might occur on plays when the foot would be employed in the football game. After Rentzel's stunning reception, Johnny Treadwell, the Longhorns all-American guard-linebacker, a player so intense that he always refused to smile beginning on the Thursday before the Saturday game in Dallas, noticed that an OU player was lining up incorrectly for the extra point. Treadwell plunged through the gap and blocked the kick, effectively removing the exclamation point after the Sooner "TD!"

The Longhorns won the game, 9–6, but for a team with national-championship ambitions, that score didn't look good on their résumé. Looney was the game's leading rusher, and by now he had taken on the punting job, too, and got off a sixty-yard orbit shot. Afterward, the Sooners were bummed, not only because they'd lost the game, but because they were now convinced that the better team didn't win. They felt that Texas was lucky, and some—like Monte Deere, the quarterback—said so.

The game ended in a brawl between the teams, an uncommon event for the Texas-OU game. Joe Don Looney did not get involved in that, most likely because the OU bench didn't provide a jukebox and an open bar.

So the two teams went their separate paths, Texas to the Cotton Bowl and Oklahoma to the Orange. The Sooners won

the Big Eight, with Looney leading the conference in rushing and the country in punting. Bud Wilkinson was less than happy with the overall aspect of Looney as the student athlete. "I hate going to class," Looney told the coach. "It interferes with going to get my laundry."

A veteran reporter and journalist, Michael Wallis, wrote a memoir of his forty years of touring the Midwest, entitled *Route 66: The Mother Road.* Wallis said that the two characters who stood out most vividly on that career path were Pretty Boy Floyd and Joe Don Looney. In the OU locker room, laundry barrels were labeled "Shirts," "Jocks," etc., and the reporter noticed that Looney had tossed his shirt into what was clearly identified as the sock barrel. The AP man asked Looney why he did that, and Looney said, "No goddamn sign is going to tell *me* what to do."

Both Texas and OU were shut out in their bowl games, the Longhorns by LSU, the Sooners by an Alabama team that had Joe Namath and Lee Roy Jordan on the field and Bear Bryant on the sidelines. President John Kennedy attended that game in Miami and visited both teams before the kickoff. Looney missed that. He was back in the john, bellowing with the wet heaves.

New Year's Day was forgotten at once in Austin and Norman because the table was being set for what was to be the biggest and loudest collision—to date—in the annals of the series.

Red Candle Day

Joe Don Looney arrived at my apartment on a Friday night in late August 1963, and he was bearing a gift. It was a case of Jax beer that he had brought back from a summer conditioning trip to Baton Rouge, and he'd already knocked off easily a fourth of it by the time he arrived at my place. He'd prepared for the season by participating in LSU's storied bodybuilding program, and he had written a letter to the Oklahoma coaching staff informing them that instead of reporting at the desired 210 that OU trainers had recommended, he would show up for two-a-day workouts at closer to 240. He had declined to also disclose that he was faster than he'd been the previous season—he'd let the coaches discover that for themselves. His neck was now the approximate circumference of an average-size trailer-park housewife's thigh.

Looney was intent on watching the 1963 College All-Star game, an event that featured the collegiate all-Americans from the previous season against the defending champions of the National Football League. It was a game that annually signaled the beginning of the football season. The pros almost always won. Looney was intent on seeing the game because he knew that in one year's time, he'd be playing in it.

Sometime during the first half, a voice from inside the television set belonging to Chris Schenkel began reading a promo for ABC's coverage of the upcoming season. The big game, Schenkel told the audience, might come early—"when the defending national champions, the USC Trojans, host Oklahoma and its explosive halfback Joe Don Looney."

Looney smiled the smile of a self-assured man. He said he was a little bit sorry that the USC game appeared so early on the Sooners' schedule. "After we kick their ass, the rest of the season will be an anticlimax," he assured me. "The Big Eight ain't got much to offer."

"What about Texas?" I asked him. The fact that he left the Austin Institute for Fun, Fellowship, and Higher Learning under less-than-auspicious circumstances—even though he refused to admit it—had become an incendiary catalyst in Looney's motivational format. His contempt had been fermenting for nearly three years. No player on the OU roster would take the field in the game in Dallas carrying a deeper grudge for the men in orange than Looney would. When I mentioned the Longhorns, Looney's eyebrows arched into sharp Vs that made him look like the Emperor Ming in those early black-and-white Flash Gordon serials, and his lips formed themselves into a double-ess sneer.

"Texas? Texas? Next time Bob Hope entertains the troops at Christmastime, he ought to take the Texas team with him. Everybody will die laughing. They're one of the greatest comedy acts of all time." Anybody who ever spent time around Looney knew that he liked to emphasize his points with phrases like that.

"Tell you what," he went on. "I'll give you Texas and twenty-one points and betcha a hundred bucks."

Now here was a genuinely tempting proposition. According to the numerical standards in place in that era, those twenty-one points were one hell of a lot of points (Texas hadn't given up as many as twenty-one points in any game for the previous five years), and $100 was a *hell* of a lot of dough. To me at least. I didn't make that much in a week as a part-time sportswriter at the *Fort Worth Press*. I gave the proposition serious thought, knowing one thing for sure: If Looney won, he'd be kicking in my apartment door within hours after the game to collect. I opened another can of Jax, shook my head, and declined the wager. The truth was that even though Texas would be ranked in the midpack of the preseason Top 10, I didn't have much faith in the '63 Longhorns.

And among people in the area who thought they knew a lot about football, I was not alone. Ben Nix had been a second-string end on the TCU Horned Frog team in 1962. His younger brother Kent Nix would become a considerably better-known athlete, playing some at quarterback for the Bears and later starting a few games with the Steelers. You can see Kent smiling conspicuously, along with some other Bears, in background shots in the dying-jock classic flick *Brian's Song*.

But Ben, the lesser-known player, should be remembered for one thing. After Texas's Southwest Conference championship team had beaten TCU, 14–0, he told a reporter (me), "Texas is more lucky than good." A lot of players around the Southwest Conference had shared that sentiment, but Nix, in an era when speaking ill of the opponent was considered bad form, had been the only one with the guts to say so in public.

The '62 Horns had finished 9-0-1 in the regular season but won at least five games on questionable calls by the zebras and on some bounces of the football that were so opportune as to stretch credulity. After the regular season ended, team captain Pat Culpepper described his team as "criticized by many, praised by few, and defeated by none." Culpepper's eloquence was unfortunately mitigated by his team's farewell performance, when the

Longhorns were outclassed, pummeled, and shut out by LSU in the Cotton Bowl. Texas' flip-flop wing-T offense, without any real backfield speed, had lost its initial potent punch and was more flop than flip. Entering the '63 campaign, Coach Darrell Royal's team was a questionable preseason conference favorite, though there was not a team on the league schedule—Texas Tech, Arkansas, Rice, SMU, Baylor, TCU, and finally mortal-blood-foe Texas A&M—whose players were not entirely solid in their conviction that they would, in the vernacular of that time and place, kick the continental dogshit out of Texas. The Longhorns had been beating these teams, mostly in tight, low-scoring games, for five years, and in the minds of the avid followers of the Aggies, Bears, et al., retribution time was at hand.

When this collection of UT seniors had arrived on campus three autumns earlier, Austin sportswriter Lou Maisel told Royal that the group offered genuine potential. Royal responded with one of his patented parables etched in time-honored, old-school Dust Bowl realities, how the best-laid plans can be ruined by plague, locust, and undue optimism. That group, now entering their final senior campaign, experienced an unbeaten freshman season and had participated in exactly two losing games in their varsity careers. In '61 and '62, the Longhorns had mounted the top rung of the AP and UPI rankings but had not stayed there long. In the minds of most of the nation, a Southwest Conference representative had no business being slotted there in the first place. Fans were suspicious that football in Texas would be regarded as a legitimate enterprise. These teams—the Michigans, the Tennessees, the Penn States, the Ohio States—did have gigantic linemen whose names all ended in -kowski, who went to college on scholarships so they wouldn't have to spend a lifetime of labor in the mills and the mines like their fathers had. Hell. There weren't any mills or mines in Texas.

At the close of the 1959 season, *Sports Illustrated* had run a story headlined "The Realm of Honest Abe." Honest Abe was Abe Martin, the TCU coach whose teams were tops in the league through the mid- to late fifties, when Royal's teams were just beginning to emerge. The article explained that Baylor was a Baptist college in a place called Waco, and that Rice was a school for eggheads in Houston that was named after Howard Hughes's ex-father-in-law, and that Texas A&M was . . . well, nobody was sure what that place was. The tone of the story was that of a *National Geographic* article depicting lifestyles of the aborigine encampments in the distant reaches of the Outback.

The hope and notion that the Longhorns or any one of these teams could or should win a national championship out of a godforsaken place like the Southwest was a distant one. A national title was not Coach Darrell Royal's primary concern entering the 1963 campaign. He just hoped to post a winning season.

His inventory of talent was not impressive. UT linemen were prawnlike when compared to the pachyderms that characterized the teams from the Rust Belt and the West Coast, where the schools played real football. Few, if any, of the skill-position players could crack 5.0 in the forty-yard dash. The team, of course, was whiter than the Confederate generals' staff. So was the whole league, for that matter, along with the Southeastern Conference. But the fact was that very few of the major colleges in America at that time carried more than two or three black players on their teams, and a quota system was strictly in place even at the Stanfords and Notre Dames of the land.

Royal's best senior was quarterback Duke Carlisle, a product of Carthage, a smallish community buried in the pine-tar obscurity of East Texas. Carlisle was a decent and slick ball handler, but a scatter-armed passer. That was okay in the Royal system. Royal regarded the forward pass as an instrument of the devil. His most-quoted theory of coaching—that business about how three things can happen when you put the ball in the air, and two of them are bad—with quarterbacks like Carlisle, the good thing that might happen would have been a roughing-the-passer call.

At the beginning of the fall semester, Carlisle's frequent social companion was a lot better known around the campus. Penny Lee Rudd had just finished as second runner-up to Miss Ohio Jacquelyn Mayer in the Miss America Pageant, seen by 60 million viewers on CBS. Penny was a UT Tri Delt, one of the top three sororities on the campus. According to UT tradition, the Kappas were rich and smart, the Tri Delts were rich and perky, and the Pi Phis were just rich. A cheerleader in '63, Kay Bailey was a typical Kappa. She currently serves in the United States Senate. (Duke and Penny would get married, but Penny would later divorce Duke and marry Vic Damone, the singer.)

The Longhorns did have a few factors working in their favor entering the season. First, their opening three games were against three teams—Tulane, Texas Tech, and Oklahoma State—that would offer modest competition. Second, Darrell Royal's teams always stayed remarkably injury-free. That factor was presumably due to superior conditioning, but the truth was the players would prefer to play hurt rather than enter the sadistic—diabolical, according to some—rehab program run by the team's trainer Frank Medina. The football players regarded Medina as the epitome of evil. But Royal's entire organizational plan was geared to the notion that football is no place for the weak or physically impaired. And when the coach said that football doesn't build character, it merely eliminates the weak, he wasn't offering a philosophical aside. There was no sympathy, much less condolences and cold lemonade, for the wounded. A candidate for the team in the late 1950s, Robert Spellings, recalls the joys of football practice. Spellings—whose wife Margaret Spellings (at this writing) is the United States Secretary of Education—had been an all-city end in high school and a track star in Fort Worth. "Then in a scrimmage, somebody rolled into me from the side, and my left leg was crushed. The trainers were already tending to somebody who'd been knocked out a couple of plays earlier, and I was groveling on the practice field in agony," Spellings recalls his last official day as a UT football player. "One of the coaches leaned over to me and said, 'Can you get up?' I told him that I couldn't, so he just nodded and moved the scrimmage about ten yards away from where I was lying, just so nobody would trip over me until they dragged me off."

Medina's sadistic practices would be publicized a decade later in the bestselling *Meat on the Hoof: The Hidden World of Texas Football* (St. Martin's, 1972) by former UT gridder Gary Shaw, in which he summed it up succinctly: "They raise cattle and football players in Texas. The cattle are treated better." There are plenty of players at UT who got hurt and will confirm that the author of *Meat on the Hoof* did have a legitimate beef, and while football players at Texas did tend to date prettier women than most, the cattle didn't have to attend class and participate in off-season conditioning programs.

When Texas opened its 1963 season, the first three games were a breeze, as expected. Texas won those, 25–0, 49–7, and 36–7, over Tulane, Texas Tech, and Oklahoma State, respectively. But the injury factor, the alleged plus, backfired. Fullback Ernie Koy, the only back on the team with any real pro potential, tore up a shoulder against Oklahoma State and was gone for the season—this, the week before the epic collision in Dallas against the Oklahoma Sooners. This subtraction from the lineup was particularly damaging because Koy, the punter, had a cannon for a right leg, booming forty-five yarders on average. In Royal's most optimistic pregame scenario, the match would be a close one, decided in the end by the kicking units.

OU had beaten Southern Cal, the defending national champion and favorite to repeat, on national television, just like Joe Don Looney predicted it would. The game was played in Santa Ana–like wind conditions—one hundred and eighteen degrees—and Looney ran nineteen yards for an early touchdown, helping the Sooners win, 17–12. The Sooners had offensive weapons other than Looney as well. Larry Shields, a single wing tailback from a state championship team at Wichita Falls, was emerging as a sophomore star, living up to his ample "stud hoss" reputation. OU also returned an all–Big Eight fullback, Jim Grisham, from Olney, Texas, one of those Tornado Alley towns that also is home to the state's only dove shoot limited to one-armed hunters. End John Flynn was another all–Big Eight returnee. Looney, after he arrived at OU in the fall of 1962, identified Flynn as probably his best friend on the team. That figured. After an OU-Missouri game, Dan Devine, the Tigers' coach, wrote a letter to the league commissioner suggesting that John Flynn's style of play should merit a lifetime banishment from the sport of football.

Texas, though unbeaten and ranked number two, was a touchdown underdog going into the game. (Frankly, I was glad I'd refused Looney's twenty-one-point proposition. And if I'd known a little bit more about football at the time, I would have known that Royal's team would come to Dallas armed with incentive of its own and would be immaculately prepared to play.)

Pat Culpepper, the all-American linebacker from the '62 team who'd lamented the absence of respect that his team had garnered, was still in Austin as an assistant coach. Culpepper and two other Longhorns, lineman David McWilliams and line-backer Timmy Doerr, all came from Cleburne, a smallish community south of Forth Worth. (During World War II, German POWs lived in a camp there. The Cleburne-ites were upset because the POWs received a daily beer ration and the townspeople didn't.)

The three Cleburne boys represented that type of football player now long extinct: the sub-two-hundred-pounder. If you saw them on the street, they'd pass for college students. These were the types of players that Royal was sending into the trenches, though. Instinctive football players. The on-the-field thinking types that Bud Wilkinson coveted.

The key to victory was don't outweigh 'em . . . outwit 'em. Culpepper knew that Royal and his staff were concocting something that might render the Sooners somewhat less invincible than advertised. The Texas-OU game was always a nightmare for offensive coaches, simply because the defenses on both teams hit the Cotton Bowl so hyped up, so insanely eager to maim, kill, and destroy anything that stepped in their way, that these whirlwind defenses were virtually impossible to block. "Most players on both defenses, you couldn't stop them with a .30-caliber bullet," Culpepper said. Still, Royal had intently studied the Sooners defenders, knew what OU would anticipate, and came up with a strategy to catch the Sooners off guard. Royal decided to split his left end, Pete Lammons, wider than the conventional lineup, and he brought wingback Phil Harris inside and positioned him in the slot. With OU looking to stop UT's version of the Green Bay Packers' patented power sweep, Royal instead would come at them with weak-side option plays from his adjusted formation.

The OU-week atmosphere around Austin was bubbling from simmer to full boil. Students were resorting to voodoo, if that's what it took to beat the Sooners. Madam Hipple, an Austin psychic who had enjoyed the full faith of UT coeds for two generations, had suggested in 1940 that Texas could upset Texas A&M if Austinites would burn red candles. It worked, too, and twenty-three years later, the candles were gleaming again across the Texas Hill Country. Royal remained dubious. On his weekly TV show, the coach said, "It's going to take more than red candles to stop Joe Don Looney." Now Royal didn't say so, but he was suspicious that while the candles might not do the job, he had a couple of players on his defense who absolutely could.

Tackle Scott Appleton, Royal and his assistants realized, would be a force that could defeat any OU lineman. He was a kind of player seldom seen on college playing fields those days— the product of a small town. Because good athletes in little schools would play every sport, including tennis, and then work for the volunteer fire department on weekends, the small school could not concentrate on being a good sports school. Plus, all of those hick programs had crappy weight programs.

Appleton was the product of Brady, Texas, which is the site of the state's finest and best goat cookoff. If deer hunting were an Olympic event, Texas could secede from the union and win the gold medal every four years, and if the Pro Football Hall of Fame is in Canton, Ohio, then the deer hunting Hall of Fame could only be situated in Brady. Pickup trucks in the town are adorned with antlers, inside and out, and Pat Culpepper recalled visiting the area with Appleton. "Scott stopped his car and shot a deer right off the highway," Culpepper said, "and a game warden saw that and chased us all the way to Junction." (Guns were big in the lives of many players in the UT-OU rivalry. Looney himself owned a damn arsenal, and if there was any facet of frat life at UT in which he truly fit in, that was it. That Kappa Sig house was a David Koresh wet dream.) But with OU week on the horizon, Appleton converted his enthusiasms to Sooners hunting and was setting some pregame traps.

"Mike Campbell [UT defensive coach and maestro of tactical intricacies] had prepared his game plan for the OU game and drawn it onto a blackboard before a team meeting," Culpepper said, "and Scott came in before the meeting, erased the whole scheme, and replaced it with the Brady High School defense, with Appleton at middle linebacker."

Campbell, naturally, was not amused, nor was he particularly disturbed, because he already had a middle linebacker whom he liked, and it wasn't Scott Appleton. San Antonio sophomore Tommy Nobis wasn't just bowlegged, his legs resembled a pair of pliers. But neither Mike Campbell nor Royal nor anybody else associated with the UT program could remember having seen such an out-and-out defensive killing machine.

"Bowlegged, but my God, he was fast," recalls Culpepper, "and never faster than in his sophomore season, before he had all those knee operations that would slow him down as a pro. The Oklahoma offense was confident coming into the Dallas game, and they had a right to be. But they [OU] really had no inkling of how good Tommy Nobis was. After the season, pro scouts told us that they all thought Tommy was better than Dick Butkus."

The Texas team that put on its coat-and-tie road outfit and boarded the charter airliner for the one-hour flight up to Dallas was prepared, but scarcely brimming with confidence. As usual, the Longhorns were quartered at the Melrose Hotel on Oak Lawn Avenue in Dallas. The Melrose, staid and proper—and customarily the home of casts of traveling Broadway productions that came to perform in the summer musicals—called its bar the Library. Friday night before the game, the Texas players attended the movies—those being films of the Oklahoma football team. These film sessions were for players only, since the coaching staff was scattered throughout the Dallas–Fort Worth area scouting Friday-night high school football talent. After absorbing the OU films, the players strolled the front sidewalks of the Melrose. The hotel was removed by at least two miles from the downtown pregame hysterics. The players, though, could see the dazzling Dallas skyline and, from the streets, could hear the hair-raising symphonic din of the ceaseless blaring of automobiles honking and could palpably feel the throbbing rages of the riotous intoxic-ites. (Not all of the pregame grotes-queries happened downtown. At the Theatre Lounge strip club on Greenville Avenue, a couple of the dancers were performing, as a tribute to the football visitors, routines featuring Sooner Nooner and Hornie Hookums.)

Beyond downtown, to the south, a Friday-night college game was being played. SMU was a big underdog against the Naval Academy, but the Ponies pulled off an upset based around the explosive runs of a track guy now going out for the football team. That was John Roderick, the same guy who'd showed off his .45 automatic to Joe Don Looney at the high school regional meet. The Longhorns were hardly overjoyed to hear the out-come of the SMU-Navy game. If there was going to be an upset in Dallas that weekend, it was going to involve the Longhorns, not the Ponies.

The team then retired for the night, where Medina, no lon-ger the brutal, whip-wielding czar of team toughness, had pre-pared for bedtime snacks. The game-day morning routine went as usual, with Royal again distributing his kicking sheets and imploring every player to remain diligent to the little details involved with making the special teams special. Then the players climbed on the buses for the trip to the State Fair grounds and the Cotton Bowl. Every player now realized that he would soon be involved in two fights, one against the crimson-shirted Okies and another, the harder battle, being the one within, in which the player had to reject the all-too-human instinct to quit when the body transmits signals that it can take no more.

Finally, game time arrived. Texas took the opening kickoff and right away took advantage of the weak-side option play that Royal had installed especially for the anticipated froth-around-the-lips aggressions of the OU defense. Carlisle took the Longhorns on a sixty-seven-yard scoring march. I was sitting in the end zone, and while they don't call 'em the cheap seats for nothing, there was an interesting view of the way the plays were developing on the field. When Texas ran the weak-side option, the OU defense took on the look of a picket fence with a slat missing. Carlisle jumped into the gaps for big gainers, working with the adeptness of a skillful cosmetic surgeon, taking a nip here and a tuck there. He finally scored from the one. Then Texas employed a defensive tactic that the Sooners hadn't seen. Looney was a diesel locomotive of a ball carrier, not a high-stepping gazelle. The Texas scheme was to not attempt a tackle above the ankles. It worked. Looney was tripped play after play. It was his prodigious punting efforts that kept the game close. Mike Campbell's UT defense, with Appleton defying the Oklahoma blocking scheme, choked off the Sooners' attack wherever they attempted to go. A fourteen-yard touchdown run by Texas tailback Tommy Ford propelled UT into a 14–0 halftime lead, and the Longhorns were not going to relent. Their first-half successes triggered some trash talk directed toward the frustrated Sooners. UT captain David McWilliams put a stop to that. "Shut the hell up," he chastised a teammate. "You're liable to wake them up."

The awakening never took place, and Texas won, 28–7—the team's most heralded postwar victory, and probably the biggest in the history of the school. Afterward, Royal could have viewed the stats and credited the win to his passing attack. Texas threw the ball exactly three times (completing one) against Oklahoma—definitely Darrell's kind of game.

Looney offered this explanation: "They kicked the shit out of us. I think we were too cocky."

The Sooners never understood that the red candle spell had zapped their bodily essences. Staley Faulkner, a first-string tackle from Denton who descended from a tribe (we all come from tribes) that was good at pushing heavy things around and probably built Stonehenge, figured that something was wrong with the Sooners players, something he couldn't quite identify. "Maybe," Faulkner said, "Coach Royal ought to give the game ball to the fucking fortune-teller."

Any respect that Texas, now number one in the land, might have earned in that Dallas coup didn't last long. The Monday after the OU game, Sooners coach Bud Wilkinson kicked Looney off the team. It was cited that during the off week before the prior game Looney had fought with a student in practice and that Looney had mostly been screwing off in practice, anyway— thus creating bad morale. The implication was that the team Texas had beaten was not the real OU. Bud Wilkinson said so himself, in his weekly newsletter dispatched to the OU followers. "Obviously, they [UT] are a better team, but the disappointing fact remains that we failed to use our best abilities. When you lose and make an all-out effort, you are never satisfied, but at least you can say that you went down with your guns blazing and flags flying. It's not a disgrace to lose this way. But when a team loses without preparing to the best of its ability and without playing at its greatest effort—particularly in a vitally important national championship game—you cannot help but pause, reflect and wonder why." So how can one not help but conclude that Wilkinson paused, reflected, quit wondering why, and gave Joe Don the bum's rush? Looney's version of what happened (related to me at the time) went like this: "Bud was eating out the team at lunch on Monday. He was pissed off because some of them were smoking on the bus going to the game, and then he said, 'And by the way, I've had it with [John] Flynn and Looney. They're gone.' So I ran into Flynn on campus, and he said, 'Have you heard the news? We've been kicked off the team.' So I went back to the dorm, packed up, and drove home to Fort Worth. I found out the next day that while I was packing, Flynn had gone to Bud and gotten his deal worked out." Flynn never left the team.

For the remainder of the 1963 season, Oklahoma went through the motions of playing out its Big Eight schedule. The Sooners had entered the season geared to the proposition that the season would amount to a national championship or nothing. Now the team was living life with the latter alternative. Though he insisted on denying it, a Sooners fan might ponder the possibility that Wilkinson's focus was directed toward his political career, not so much on the football team. In Bud Wilkinson's last game as the head coach of the Oklahoma Sooners, OU—the best trained, best disciplined team of that era—in the process of losing to Nebraska, turned the ball over six times in the second half.

Back in Austin, the Longhorns were coping with the burden of the target that always marked the number one team in the nation at midseason. The Oklahoma game had been one of those occasions where the stars were aligned and the pieces fit. Royal realized that the breaks were not always there week to week. OU weekend was a figment of the past. Without Ernie Koy, Texas lacked the firepower to dominate Southwest Conference defenses. Texas beat Arkansas, 17–12, but was hardly impressive. Same the next week, a listless 10–6 win over Rice. A pattern was established. Texas, in each of its games, had scored a touchdown on its opening drive and then circled the wagons. Once Texas got the lead, Campbell's defensive units played as conservatively as the UT offense. Texas would seldom blitz. Holding a one-TD edge, Campbell wanted to avoid yielding any big plays.

Next was SMU. (Two years earlier, Lee Iacocca had watched SMU play against the Michigan Wolverines and was impressed by the feisty little Texans, even though they lost, and decided to call his new sporty little Ford the Mustang.)

During pregame warm-ups before the Texas game, SMU captain Billy Gannon approached a Texas halfback, Joe Dixon, who was catching punts, and said, "Joe, we're getting ready to kick your fucking ass." Gannon was the product of Dallas's highfalutin Highland Park High School, like his fast teammate John Roderick.

Gannon's pregame pronouncement failed to occur, but barely. Texas jumped out to a quick lead, then went into its defensive posture. This was Royal's season-long tactic. It was ideal for World Cup soccer but hardly something to gain the approval of the voters of the AP Top Ten. The Horns hung on to beat SMU, 17–13. After the game, the Texas team bus rolled away from the Cotton Bowl and happened to pass Billy Gannon, walking arm in arm with his girlfriend. Gannon shot the Longhorns the finger. That simple gesture seemed to represent the feelings of America's football fans toward Darrell Royal and his number one Longhorns.

Still, spirits were high among the student ranks at UT. Of course, they were always high. Magazines such as *Playboy* and *Penthouse* used to run stories that identified the great American party schools. UT usually ranked even higher in that category than it did in the football polls. Colorado and Wisconsin were its bitterest rivals. Here's what the magazine people didn't understand: UT was not a party school; it was a let's-blow-off-class-and-go-soak-in-some-rays school. The whole Austin area is blessed with an abundance of lakes and creeks and spring-fed pools, surrounded by grassy areas that provide a welcoming quality that compels a person to want to lie down. Nobody in slacker-land city took the world too seriously, because if they did, they might wind up being a lobbyist.

The week following the SMU game, Texas beat Baylor in another close contest, 7–0. It appeared Baylor had tied the game in the final minute on a pass from Don Trull to his wide-open all-American end Lawrence Elkins, but Carlisle (this was the final year of the one-platoon era of college football) materialized out of nowhere to leap in front of Elkins and intercepted the ball in the end zone. The next game was against TCU. These were the same people who had agitated Royal into trotting out that vintage Okie-ism about the bunch of cockroaches. Texas avoided the upset this time and won, 17–0. But this TCU team had been etched in mediocrity all year, and the 17–0 win, again, was not the stuff of a national championship team.

Texas had an off week before its regular-season finale against the Texas Aggies. On Friday, the team was eating lunch in the athletic dining room at Moore-Hill Hall when word arrived from Dallas that John Kennedy had been assassinated. The following Sunday, when Jack Ruby barged into the basement of Dallas police headquarters and shot Lee Harvey Oswald, right there on live television, hundreds of Texas and Oklahoma football fans were horrified. "My God! That's the same awful place they took me in the paddy wagon the night before the '59 game, when I got arrested for throwing that quart bottle of malt liquor through the plate-glass window at Neiman Marcus!"

A mood of intense anti-Texas fervor took over the country. One reporter on CBS said that the most shocking thing was that the president was murdered in such "a remote part of the country," implying that Texas might as well have been Azerbaijan.

So a pall was cast over Texas's already dubious claim to the national football top spot. And on Thanksgiving against the Aggies, playing on national television before a huge captive audience since the Detroit Lions game (also always on Thanksgiving) was already over, the Longhorns seemed out of synch, if not lifeless. Playing in the mud, they fell behind 13–3 but managed a comeback only because of a dumb Aggie play. An A&M player made what should have been the upset-sealing interception late in the game, but then he attempted to lateral the ball. He fumbled it, just like Reggie Bush would in that Rose Bowl game of 2006. Texas recovered and finally won, 15–13, when Carlisle sneaked it over. Now Texas faced Navy quarterback and Heisman Trophy winner Roger Staubach in the Cotton Bowl. Texaphobia was rampant throughout the land. Myron Cope, a columnist from Pittsburgh, said that Navy would destroy Texas, "a team populated by slow guys with skinny legs and big butts." Everyone got the picture. Slow. Slow and white. (It should be historically noted here that the Naval Academy team in 1963 was just as white as the Longhorns. Whiter, probably, since the UT players soaked in all those Austin rays in the off-season while the Midshipmen were riding around in submarines.)

In Austin, the cartoon characters that Cope described were involved in specialized preparations for the game. Coach Mike Campbell had devised a Staubach Chase Drill, designed to prepare a scheme that might contain the quarterback. Staubach, as fast and maneuverable in his time as Vince Young would become in his, confounded defenses all year by rolling out in one direction, then reversing his field, laughingly, it seemed, eluding the pursuing defenders who'd been lured into his trap. Campbell trained his tacklers to station themselves in the areas to watch when Staubach zigged, and then to be positioned to nail him when he zagged.

Wayne Hardin, the Navy coach, had been insisting that even though Texas had already been knighted as the national champ by both major wire services, the title was bogus if the Longhorns lost to Navy. While Hardin had been actively arguing that East Coast football was superior to anything these Texans might bring to the picnic, the Longhorn coaches had figured out how to steal the defensive signals that Navy sent from the bench. Ha.

Finally, shortly before the kickoff, CBS's Lindsey Nelson placed the rival coaches side by side in the tunnel in the south end zone of the Cotton Bowl—in Dallas, now renowned worldwide as "the city of hate." He asked Coach Hardin to articulate his thoughts. "When the challenger meets the champion, and the challenger wins, then there's a new champion," he told America. Nelson asked Royal for a response.

In a clear voice, Royal's reply was succinct. "We're ready."

It wasn't what Royal said, it was how he said it—the edge in his voice that resounded without the actual words . . . *we're ready . . . to take a two-by-four to your goddamn ass. Just who the fuck do you think you are?*

Thirty-six years and two months later, I interviewed Roger Staubach for a business magazine, the topic being Staubach's huge commercial real estate company, headquartered in Dallas. Of course the conversation eventually found its way to football.

Staubach played in four Super Bowls, winning two and starring in four. The game that stood out in his mind, though, was that Texas game.

"Those Texas guys," he remembered. "They just beat the living hell out of me. People talk to me about what it was like playing against Jack Lambert and the like. The guy in my nightmares is George Brucks—from Hondo, Texas—probably didn't weigh 200 pounds. He took my head off. All day long." While Staubach was being assaulted, Texas, knowing what Navy's defense was going to do before each and every play, lofted passes over the Middies defense—Carlisle to Harris—for two quick and easy first-half touchdowns. Texas won 28–6. When the day was over, Texas was the national champion. An unlikely one. But in the end, absolutely undisputed.

Back in Norman, the Bud Wilkinson epoch came to an end. Wilkinson officially announced that he would seek a seat in the U.S. Senate, running as a Republican. His candidacy was tied to Barry Goldwater's 1964 bid for the presidency against Lyndon Johnson. Goldwater said he favored the use of American nuclear force in warfare. "In your heart, you know he's right," was Barry's campaign slogan. Oklahoma Democrats distributed thousands of bumper stickers that read "Beat Barry, Bud and Texas."

Political analysts wondered whether Wilkinson's bad loss to Texas might impact his race for the senate. One pollster estimated that the setback cost him 50,000 to 70,000 votes.

Three weeks before the November election, OU played Texas under its new coach, Bud's longtime loyal and trusted assistant, Gomer Jones. The Longhorns won by the same score as the previous year, 28–7. Afterward, Dave Campbell, a Waco sports columnist and founder of *Texas Football* magazine, wrote, "Those Oklahomans might beat Barry and Bud this year, but they'll never beat Texas, and in their hearts, they know that's right."

Wilkinson lost his bid for the senate. Of more than 900,000 votes cast, he was beaten by Fred Harris, the Democrat, by a 21,000-vote margin. If the analysts were correct, Wilkinson could thank Duke Carlisle, Tommy Nobis, Scott Appleton, et al., for the demise of his ambitions in the senate chamber. That's the law of the landscape in Sooner territory: Senators and presidents will come and go. The Texas game is forever and eternal.

7

The Austin Strangler

In most parts of Texas, the 1960s, like news of the Emancipation Proclamation, arrived late. Hippies didn't materialize on the streets of Dallas until, like, 1973.

Austin was different. All the vibes of unrest and insurrection associated with the 1960s freak movement were in place by mid-decade. Maybe not the insurrecting business, at first. But the concept of free love and drugs was greeted with wholesale applause by huge blocs of the campus population. Suddenly, instead of serenading beneath the veranda of a sorority house, some . . . (well, I know of at least one, so there must have been others) . . . of the frat boys had taken to eating six hits of windowpane acid for breakfast and were spending a lot of time in treetops. Good. Like getting drunk, if you're going to hallucinate, it's a lot healthier to do it outdoors.

Different kind of sorority girl, too. Puffin' pot, on the pill, and empowered as never before.

The freak scene did as much for Austin, Texas, on a long-term basis as any city in the world. That whole Willie Nelson "dope-smokin' goat roper" manifesto came and never left, as evidenced in the civic-spirited billboards you still see around the town: "Austin . . . Keep It Weird." To paraphrase the old U.S. Army recruiting slogan, people in Austin eat more Mexican food by nine in the morning than most people eat all day.

It needs to be remembered, though, that the Aquarian Age sweetness did not arrive in Austin upon the wings of a benign zephyr. Societal change made a jagged entry, in fact. Let's examine 1966.

First, two coeds disappeared.

Shirley Stark and Susan Rigsby. Pretty girls. Roommates. Rigsby, the daughter of Theo Rigsby, president of the Texas High School Coaches Association. After about a week, their bodies were located in a field, and finally the killer was located. UT student. Bright as hell. James Cross, from Joe Don Looney's alma mater, Paschal High School in Fort Worth.

Weeks later, the same thing happened again, this time the perp being an aspiring sportswriter for UT's *Daily Texan* who wrote about the football team. Bill White strangled his date to death after a Christmas party. She wouldn't come across, so he put his hands on her throat and didn't stop pressing until she was dead on the kitchen floor of her apartment. White's case didn't grab the headlines like the Cross murders. "I confessed right away, didn't try to hide the body, like Cross," White told me after he'd avoided the electric chair and then gotten out of the prison system entirely to write sports for a newspaper in Clearwater, Florida, having only served eight years. Good thing for White that he had been charged with murder instead of possession of three marijuana seeds. Otherwise, he'd still be locked up.

Then August 1, 1966, witnessed the coming of some of the most down-and-dirty mojo that the state would ever experience. A UT student carried a footlocker loaded with high-caliber rifles and enough ammo to storm an atoll and rode the elevator to the observation deck of the Texas library tower. He shot and killed the woman employed to discourage visitors from screwing out on the deck, then began firing away at the people on the ground beneath him.

Summer school students were pinned down and hid behind trees and benches. Others—in a situation that shouldn't be funny but is—braved the gunfire to sprint to Scholz's, Austin's most popular outdoor pub, which was offering free beer that day to celebrate its one hundredth anniversary. By the time an Austin cop, who had to rank as the bravest in the history of the planet, went out on the observation deck and killed the sniper, Charles Whitman had murdered sixteen people and wounded thirty-one others.

Naturally, I knew him.

Whitman, like me, had resided in the early 1960s on the seventh floor of the Goodall-Wooten dormitory, better known as the Goodie-Woo, on Guadalupe Street, the drag, across from the campus. This was a good place to live, a high-rise. A Catholic church and a convent were a block away. Every room in the dorm had a balcony, and you could stand out there at night with a deer rifle fitted with a high-powered scope and look through that at the nuns as they dressed for bed. The dorm manager, a retired major in the U.S. Army, used to hypnotize my roommate and me and stick big safety pins through our hands while we pretended to be locked in a trance and so couldn't feel it. Really, it hurt like hell. Why put up with that? Because in return for enduring the hypnotics, the dorm manager allowed us to keep booze in our room—basically let us do whatever the hell we wanted to, even gave me free rent in exchange for painting the stairwell. His name was Dan; he was a huge fan of the Longhorns football team, and he stood up for me big-time when this little disciplinary matter arose at the office of a certain gentleman who got paid for being a dean. The dean hated everybody who lived at the Goodie-Woo because somebody had dropped a grocery bag filled with water off a balcony and scored a bull's-eye on his wife's head.

Dan the dorm manager was a great guy, and I was disappointed to later read that he'd been involved in some murder that happened in Galveston. I don't know that Dan ever attempted to hypnotize Whitman, but I suspect that he did. Whitman was an ex-Marine cited by the corps for his ability to hit moving targets at long range. He was fond of guns, having shot a deer out of season, then gutting the animal in the bathtub of his dorm. Also, Whitman enthusiastically played high-stakes poker, almost always lost, seldom paid up, and accused everybody of cheating. After the massacre, the shrinks all said that Whitman's mean and abusive father was the cause of it all. Well, if everybody in that day and time who had a hard-ass daddy took it personally, people would have been firing away off every rooftop in Texas. Charles Whitman was a natural-born prick. End of story. And he gave the University of Texas a worldwide image as being a dangerously uncivilized place, which wasn't necessarily true.

The dark clouds of uncool karma would form menacingly over the football operation, too.

On the Friday night before Longhorn games, sports information director Jones Ramsey would rent the biggest suite at the Villa Capri motel as a media hospitality center, providing some of the nation's top sports journalists with all of the bottled hospitality they could possibly consume. Darrell Royal would make a brief appearance. Royal was as popular among the media as any sports personality probably in the history of the whole damn state because of his on-the-field success and unceasing quotability. In truth, I doubt that Royal actually liked many of the sportswriters, and he said more than once that the key to getting along with the media was simply keeping everyone's glass full.

Jones Ramsey was as good at that as anybody in the recording annals of American public relations.

Southern Cal came to Austin to play the Longhorns in the nationally televised season-opening game of the 1966 season. One of the visitors to Jones Ramsey's open-bar media-information center at the Villa Capri happened to be an ex-Trojan football player in Austin to cheer for his old team—John "I whipped cancer and I'll whip you" Wayne. And lemmee tell ya, pilgrim, for every free scotch this young sportswriter was guzzling—and I could pack it away with anybody in those days—John Wayne was pouring down five. Wayne was accompanied on his Texas visit by a man who was his wig stylist. The stylist kept telling Wayne that he didn't feel good, wanted to hit the hay. Wayne called the stylist a pussy, insisting that the man stay up and drink. Which he did, and he was found dead in his motel room the next morning.

The ill tidings carried over to the football field the next day. Texas unveiled its new quarterback, sophomore sensation Bill Bradley, who had been ordained in the media as Super Bill even before he had taken a varsity snap. Super Bill came from Palestine, the one in East Texas, not the Palestine in the Middle East, although Bradley sometimes played as if he hailed from the latter. Things had a tendency to blow up around him. Bradley ran ten yards on an option keeper on his first play as a collegian and did little the rest of the game. Southern Cal came out the winner, 10–6.

The Longhorns won their next two games against Texas Tech and Indiana. But Bradley had gotten hurt against the Hoosiers and wouldn't participate in the Oklahoma game as Texas went to Dallas hoping to extend its eight-consecutive-game dominance against the Sooners.

OU had fired the coach promoted to replace Bud Wilkinson.

Gomer Jones had fallen victim to one of the most commonplace syndromes in all of sports. Try to replace a college coaching legend, and the outcome is nearly always terminal. There are very few exceptions. Who came in at Notre Dame after Knute Rockne? Nobody remembers, because nobody could follow that act. Red Blaik left Army in the late 1950s, and I don't think they've won a game at West Point since. Same thing at Alabama, when Bear Bryant finally hung 'em up. Yeah, the Tide still plays and still wins, but everybody who's been hired to run the football operation at Tuscaloosa winds up the victim of some midnight drunkard who sticks a For Sale sign in the coach's front yard.

When Gomer Jones's 1965 team went 3-7 and lost to Oklahoma State for the first time since 1965, it was time for Gomer to leave, and he promptly resigned. To Oklahomans, that eight-game drought against Texas was as arid and distasteful as the damn Dust Bowl. Nobody had been beating the Longhorns—except Frank Broyles at Arkansas. Broyles's Razorbacks knocked off a Texas team that was ranked tops in the nation in 1964 and 1965.

So if the Sooners couldn't hire Frank Broyles, they accomplished the next best thing, bringing in Broyles's top assistant coach, Jim Mackenzie. Mackenzie brought with him another coach from the Ozarks, a bright and willing guy named Barry Switzer.

Oklahoma's Hog call was the right one. With Texas putting a subpar offense on the field—no Super Bill—Mackenzie's Sooners corralled the Longhorns and cashed in on an afternoon's worth of favorable field positions with four field goals by Mike Vachon. Meanwhile, Sooners quarterback Bob Warmack, who while quick was about the size of the average carhop in Tulsa, kept the UT defense off-balance throughout the game.

"Made us look like a bunch of fools was what he did," Texas linebacker Joel Brame said afterward. The Sooners went on to defeat the Longhorns, 18–9. This was my first newspaper assignment at a Texas-OU game, and I interviewed people in both dressing rooms afterward. Darrell Royal had been beaten at the State Fair for the first time since his first season in Austin, 1957, and he wasn't a damn bit happy about it, either. His responses to reporters' various inquiries as to what the hell had gone wrong were politely curt. I asked Royal how he'd evaluated the performance of Andy White the quarterback who'd replaced Super Bill. "Andy is a sophomore, and his inexperience showed from time to time," Royal responded, rolling his eyes as if to say, "Andy didn't play worth a crap."

On the opposite side of the famous Cotton Bowl tunnel (Royal always properly referred to it as a chute), the setting was entirely different. Coach Jim Mackenzie, full of charisma and bursting with joy, raved about the spectacle.

"First time I've seen this game, you know, and I was impressed by the crowd reaction. The stadium was full, and they were seeing the game they had talked about all winter, spring, and summer. I've played in three bowl games and coached in six others, and I've never been associated with such an enthusiastic crowd." Then Jim Mackenzie did something I'd never seen a coach do and never would again. He began to sing.

W-e-l-l-l, I don't give a damn for the whole state of T-ex-a-s-s-s . . .

I don't know if the coach actually wrote that ballad himself, but he performed the number on-key and with gusto. Jim Mackenzie was the happiest, most jubilant, most genuinely congenial professional whistle-tooter that a college football program could possibly have hired. After filing my story, I left the Cotton Bowl convinced that if Darrell Royal didn't like losing to

OU, he was going to have to get used to it because the Sooners were getting ready to roll again under Jim Mackenzie. He finished his inaugural season at 6-4 and recruited a top class prior to the 1967 season. Then, in April, I read off the UPI teletype machine that Jim Mackenzie, at age thirty-seven, had dropped dead of a heart attack.

Chuck Fairbanks was named to replace Mackenzie and was given a mandate of confidence in the form of a nine-*month* contract. The Sooners would of course press on, although three years would pass before OU would experience a bust-out season.

Texas, on the other hand, had endured two very un-Royal-like 6-4 seasons. The most recent, though, had finished with some momentum. UT had won its final three regular season games, then dominated Ole Miss in the Bluebonnet Bowl. Prior to the 1967 season, Royal was worried that the UT people were too optimistic over the outcome, and he was driving to lunch with Jones Ramsey when he saw a bumper sticker and said, "What the hell's *that*?"

The bumper sticker read: "1967—The Year of the Horns."

Royal didn't like that and, as it turned out, he had reason not to. Texas promptly lost its opener to USC, 17–13, in O. J. Simpson's maiden voyage as a college football player. The Longhorns weren't necessarily expected to beat USC, but they sure as hell were supposed to beat Texas Tech in Austin the following week. Then when they didn't, UT supporters were stuck with a very peculiar-looking Year of the Horns. Texas finally beat somebody the next week, Oklahoma State. With Super Bill Bradley providing quarterback play that was shaded by inconsistency—he was turnover prone—Royal didn't know what to expect when he took his team to Dallas to face Oklahoma.

He didn't like what he saw when he got there.

On Oklahoma's opening possession, it appeared as if the

Sooners were scrimmaging with no defense on the field. With the smallish Warmack pulling all of the right levers, OU swept seventy-eight yards in just five plays, the biggest being a forty-one-yard run through a Grand Canyon of a hole by halfback Ron Shotts. Texas was dazed. In the second quarter, the Sooners began to march again, this time behind the running of a fullback who would someday win the Heisman Trophy, Steve Owens. OU made it as far as the Texas eleven-yard line, and if they made another touchdown, then church was over.

Facing fourth and one, however, Fairbanks opted for the short field goal and summoned Vachon, hero of the 1966 season, to kick it. This time, Vachon would miss. In fact, his twenty-seven-yard effort might be remembered as the worst excuse for a placekick in the history of the Texas-OU series. Vachon not only missed the goalpost, he missed the whole damn end zone. The ball actually sailed out of bounds, and the good news for the Sooners was that Texas was forced to take over on its own three-yard line.

Down 7–0 at the half and extremely fortunate that it wasn't a lot worse, Royal chastised his team.

"There's a hell of a good fight going on out there," Royal began, *"and we ain't in it!"*

The Longhorns did participate, however, in the second half. They recovered an OU fumble and settled for a field goal after Super Bill misfired on a third-down pass. He misfired again on the first play of the fourth quarter, overthrowing receiver Ed Small, who went airborne and somehow caught the ball anyway. Bradley carried the ball in from the seven. Texas missed the extra point but held on to win oh-so-unconvincingly, 9–7. Vachon, near the end of the game, missed another short field goal that would have given the Sooners the victory. It was only a twenty-eight-yarder, but it was partially blocked. Afterward,

Royal correctly identified his team as the luckiest in the world. He was mystified by his team's lukewarm presence in the first half. "We had gotten our invitations to come and play. The game was only scheduled about thirty years ago."

Super Bill had played erratically but committed zero turnovers. OU made three, thus the difference. So Texas ended its one-game State Fair skid but would not return to the Cotton Bowl on New Year's Day for the fourth straight season. TCU's fighting cockroaches would arise to upset the Longhorns one more time, 24–17, and the Year of the Horns become the unsightliest bust since Ford unveiled the Edsel a decade earlier. Texas ended the season by losing to the Aggies, a first for Darrell Royal, and the first time the Longhorns had lost in College Station since 1951 (though almost every game was a narrow escape). Texas was down by three and driving deep into A&M territory when Bradley threw an interception. That capped UT's third straight 6-4 season, and all of a sudden the Dom Pérignon was beginning to taste like Drāno. The 10–7 loss to the Aggies was the last game that Kern Tips would ever broadcast on the Southwest Conference radio network. He died in the off-season. What a bummer.

Meanwhile, on the opposite side of the Red River, Sooners fans had been referring to Chuck Fairbanks as Fuck Chairbanks after that Texas loss, but OU regrouped nicely and won the remainder of its games, including a thriller over Tennessee in the Orange Bowl game. So old Fuck was rewarded with an extension of his nine-month contract, quelling the notion that Oklahoma might conduct a national search for a marquee name.

In Austin, during the off-season preceding the '68 season, Royal took his customary clearheaded approach to solving the Longhorns' slump: Don't get mad. Get a new offense.

Royal now had three terrific running backs. Senior-to-be

Chris Gilbert was the best halfback that Royal had coached at Texas with the possible exception of Jimmy Saxton. Another halfback, Ted Koy, was not quite as good as his older brother, Ernie, but was close. The fullback was Royal's prize bull. Sophomore Steve Worster (freshmen wouldn't be allowed to play until 1971) had been ardently recruited by all of the schools. Worster was from Bridge City, Texas, which is about as far southeast as you can get in Texas without being in Louisiana.

He'd steamrolled high school kids with such brutal efficiency that there was no question he would do the same once in college. Gilbert, Worster, and Koy made a helluva trifecta. Royal knew that and wished to employ a tactic that would enable all three to play the entire game. He instructed his offensive assistant coach, Emory Bellard, to devise college football's doomsday machine. Something diabolical. Something that would mute the critiques of the spoiled Texas fans, some of whom were beginning to bitch and whine.

Bellard—who'd coached high school football in Breckenridge, Texas, where they once actually moved some kid's house from out in the sticks to just inside the city limits so he could play for the green-clad Buckaroos—produced the blueprint for devastation that Royal had demanded. It was essentially a Y-formation, the fullback two and a half yards behind the quarterback and both halfbacks lined up behind another back, what they called the Wishbone T. Actually, Mickey Herskowitz, a Houston writer, tossed out the term and it stuck.

The quarterback, Bradley, would direct the option-oriented Wishbone. The Longhorns' new offense demonstrated ample punch in UT's home opener against the Houston Cougars. Still, the new attack engine was not fine-tuned. Worster was lined up too close to the line, taking handoffs from Bradley and hitting holes before the offensive line had time to create any. The game finished at a 20–20 standoff. The Cougars were a terrifically talented team, though. Later that season, Houston beat Tulsa 100–6, so the tie was hardly a disaster. The disaster would have to wait a week, when Texas traveled to Lubbock to play the Red Raiders, where the transmission fell out of the truck. Trailing 28–6 in the second half, Darrell Royal performed the human-resources decision that would define his coaching career: Royal benched Super Bill Bradley and replaced him with a player who was in Austin primarily because he wanted to pitch in the College World Series, and Texas was the place where you went to do that. James Street, too short to be a good college passer and just fast enough to outrun tackles and placekickers, could not bring Texas all the way back against Texas Tech. That was the last game Texas would lose until one year into the coming decade.

The Longhorns rolled past Oklahoma State just like they always did, 31–3, and that game launched a thirty-game victory streak. It was the following week, though, when the Wishbone offense would make its formal introduction on college football's main stage. The 1968 Texas-OU game was rated a toss-up. Early in the season, when Texas had misfired, OU was giving up forty-five points to Notre Dame at South Bend. The Sooners' defense would generate a more determined effort in the annual title bout in Dallas, and their collision with the suddenly potent orange Wishbone produced one of the best series ever seen. Heroes abounded on both sides, and it appeared the star of the game would be Warmack, the resourceful OU quarterback, making his third start against the Longhorns. Warmack scored with a seven-yard touchdown run with eight minutes to play, putting the Sooners ahead, 20–19. I was standing on the east sideline, waiting to do a postgame dressing room sidebar, when Warmack went in. The noise that thundered down from the stands must be what a guy hears when he goes over Niagara Falls in a barrel.

Behind James Street, Texas forged a comeback. The running game was on hold now, and Street began to throw the football. He hit his tight end, Daryl Comer, for two big gains and connected with Super Bill Bradley, now a split end, for a first down at the Oklahoma twenty-one. The clock was inching into the game's final minute. I gazed up into the stands and saw that every person inside the concrete fortress was standing, and wailing, howling, imploring. Not until *American Idol* would I again hear human beings make such a god-awful racket. Then Steve Worster won the game. He ran fourteen yards on a draw play. Texas was close enough for a Happy Feller (yes, that was his real name, just like the Georgia Bulldogs' placekicker in the Cotton Bowl game two years earlier, Happy Dicks) field goal. Texas wouldn't need Happy. One more time, the ball went to Worster. Running straight ahead, he blasted through a hole and, once inside the five, launched himself into a headfirst dive with the ball cradled in both arms, landing exactly on top of the goal line for the winning TD.

Players on both teams were totally gassed afterward, still gasping, some of them, when the reporters came to hear what they might have to say. Tackle John Titsworth had been perhaps OU's best defender, and he conceded that effort-wise, the Sooners had not left anything out on the field. "We played a little harder, I guess, just because they're Texas."

Steve Casteel, Sooners linebacker, dropped an interception on UT's scoring drive, and he was sick. "Sure, it hurts to lose," he said. "But they know they were in a ball game." That they did, and the Longhorns would not experience the sensation of competing in what amounted to a close football game for another season and a half. Texas flattened everything in its path for the remainder of the 1968 season. Against Baylor, all four backs in the Longhorn Wishbone rushed for at least one hundred yards. UT avenged the Aggie loss from the previous year, 35–14, then played in the Cotton Bowl as the SWC champ for the first time in five years, stomping the Tennessee Vols, 36–13. Street was the catalyst. His snap-judgment operation of the offense and brazen confidence offered an element of flash and dash that hadn't been seen in the Texas football program since the days of Bobby Layne. After Texas had won the pregame coin toss in the Cotton Bowl game against the Vols, the referee asked the Longhorns' captain whether his team wished to kick or receive, or defend either the north or south end zone. The captain responded, "We really don't give a damn."

After the season, Street became a team leader in another facet of football life. With the Austin campus adhering to the hippie route, Street grew sideburns and let his hair grow down over his collar. "I think it's time that we encourage James to visit a barbershop," a UT assistant coach suggested to Royal. "Or maybe we ought to start growing ours long, too," Royal came back.

The 1969 Longhorn attack was an even better version of the one that had devoured everything that tried to get in its way the previous season. Chris Gilbert had spent his eligibility and was replaced at halfback by somebody even better, sophomore Jim Bertelsen.

ABC, which was the only network televising NCAA football, realized that Texas seemed unstoppable, looked at Arkansas's schedule, and then convinced the teams to move their annual midseason game to December. That way the network could promote a possible meeting of two unbeaten teams at the end of the season—playing a national title game created of, for, and by the entertainment industry. It was ABC's Roone Arledge who concocted the scheme, the same man who further convinced his network that *NFL Monday Night Football* would work as well.

The only obstacle that might ruin this college TV dream game was Oklahoma. The Sooners could be formidable. Fullback Steve Owens was a running threat, and he would go on to win his Heisman that season. Even more troubling to the UT defense was the presence of sophomore quarterback Jack Mildren, from Abilene, Texas, the most coveted high school recruit in the nation in 1969.

Game-time temperature in Dallas for the mid-October bloodbath was ninety-three degrees, and from the outset, it was the Longhorns who were feeling the heat. Mildren made a touchdown to give OU the early lead, and the gap widened after Steve Zabel snatched a Street pass intended for the tight end, and that set up the Owens TD that put the Sooners on top, 14–0. Street, unrattled, watched from the sidelines and told his split receiver, Cotton Speyrer, to get ready to start catching the ball. It had been Street's passing that enabled Texas to come back against the Sooners in '68, and the cocky, irrepressible QB was back at it again. His TD pass to Speyrer cut the lead to 14–7, and the Longhorns never looked back. Despite throwing three interceptions, Street passed for 215 yards, and Oklahoma was finally subdued, 27–17. Chuck Fairbanks did not say so at the time, but it was after this game that he decided it was time for OU to install a Wishbone offense of its own.

As the season continued to move toward the battle of unbeaten teams, it was neither Texas nor Arkansas that topped the wire-service polls near the end. Woody Hayes's Ohio State Buckeyes were defending national champs. Equipped with talent like quarterback Rex Kern, fullback Jim Otis and his backup, John Brockington, and defensive nightmare Jack Tatum, the Buckeyes were deemed unstoppable.

I was sitting in the press box at Memorial Stadium in Austin, before Texas's game against TCU, and a writer from a Houston paper came to me and said I was the only media person in the country, evidently, who had seen both Texas and Ohio State play in person. I'd gone to Columbus in September to watch the Buckeyes dismantle TCU, 62–0. So which team—UT or OSU— would have won if those two had played?

My answer came in the form of a shrug. Hard to say. It was even harder to say after the Texas-TCU game. UT beat the Frogs 69–7, so both teams were sixty-two points better than TCU. Not that it mattered because while the Horns were boot-stomping the hell out of the Christians, Ohio State got beat by Michigan. Now the Texas-Arkansas game would match number one versus number two, and ABC's prayers were answered. This was a game that might live in history, and that came to pass.

Playing in the most hostile of possible environments in Fayetteville, and in bad weather, Texas got behind 14–0, and the situation grew grimmer by the minute in the second half. The Longhorns would rally behind Street, just like they always did, to go ahead, 15–14. Arkansas mounted a last-ditch drive behind its quarterback, Texan Bill Montgomery, advancing into Texas territory. Then Montgomery threw a sideline pass into a cluster of players. Chris Schenkel, doing the play-by-play for ABC, was confused. He couldn't figure out who had the football. It was the Longhorns' grand old foe, Bud Wilkinson, handling the color, who delivered the joyful tidings to UT fans.

"It's intercepted," Wilkinson said simply. End of game.

Richard Nixon entered the UT dressing room afterward, where he decreed that the Longhorns were the overlords of all of college football. As Nixon prepared to leave, one of the UT players shouted, "Thank you, Mr. President!"

"You deserve it," said Nixon.

"No," the player countered, "I'm thanking you for the high number I got in the [military] draft lottery."

UT's New Year's date was a stunner. Notre Dame decided to participate in a bowl game for the first time since the 1927 Rose Bowl game, when the Irish had the Four Horsemen. So after all those years, the Irish, under coach Ara Parseghian, decided the time was right to reenter the postseason. At the annual Cotton Bowl luncheon, Texas governor Preston Smith stood and welcomed "Coach Parz-a-gans" and our visitors "from the great state of Eel-a-noise." Parseghian, ever so cool, responded, "Thank you, Governor Schmidt."

The game greeted the dawning of a new decade. The Irish, behind quarterback Joe Theisman, did not come to Dallas for the purpose of getting beat. Just as they had against Arkansas, UT trailed most of the game, then rallied to win after Street connected on a crucial fourth-down pass inside the Irish ten-yard line. Officials had to bring out the chains to determine if Texas had made its first down. It had, by about one link. Texas won, 21–17, and the UT dressing room was a mob scene. I counted three celebrities in there—singer Trini Lopez, actor Fess Parker, and politician Lyndon Johnson. Poor guy. Out of office and unloved by all. Just to cheer Johnson up, I asked him for an autograph, the first and last time that would happen in my life. He scrawled "LBJ" across the back of a stat sheet.

The win over Notre Dame put Royal at the pinnacle of his career. He would never enjoy a better day. People around the state were encouraging Royal to think about running for governor himself.

Royal, remember, had seen the motion picture *Giant* the night before he had interviewed for the coaching job at Texas. In a social occasion in the summer of 1970, in California, I was talking with one of the actors in that film, Chill Wills, and mentioned the talk of Royal in the Governor's Mansion. Old Chill—his face turned the color of an OU home-game jersey. He pounded his glass of bourbon onto a table and muttered in that gravelly voice of his, "N-o-o-o-o. Huh-uh. Not gonna happen. Darrell is too fine a person to get mixed up in something like politics."

Everything associated with that Notre Dame game seemed to turn to gold. The story that I wrote for the *Press* won a big award that they presented at this black-tie deal, and Walter Cronkite gave it out. Writing about James Street, my first paragraph read: "As the cannibal found out after he ate the missionary, you can't keep a good man down."

The lasting legacy that football historians bring to the fore regarding the original Texas Wishbone is that the team picture is whiter than the Vienna Boys Choir. Black players did not appear in Southwest Conference football games until 1966, when Jerry Levias began his career at SMU. Texas was the last team in the league, or probably anywhere else in college football, to put a black in uniform.

I was the first sportswriter in Fort Worth to offer any kind of coverage to the black high schools in Fort Worth. This was in 1963, when the papers devoted two paragraphs maximum to the Negro (correct term du jour) games. The schools were still completely segregated. Before long, I'd be talking to an administrator of a well-known Texas college about this color barrier, and he would say, in his real syrupy East Texas preacher voice, "Well, My-uck. Yew know, we'd love to take some, but we jist can't git 'em in school."

Two writers from the *Press* sports section began to champion the cause of James Cash, a basketball player at I. M. Terrell, a black high school in Fort Worth. TCU's coach, Buster Brannon, gave him a scholarship. Cash, on the basketball court, actually preceded Levias on the football field, and he led the Frogs to the conference championship his senior year. Yes, somehow TCU managed to keep Cash in school. And what would become of him? Well, the poor dumb bastard wound up as the dean of the Harvard MBA program.

8

The Whoosh-Bone

The bus rolls toward the stadium, drawing ever closer to the thundering abyss that lies within the gray walls of the Cotton Bowl. There's still maybe a couple of miles to the Grand Avenue entrance to the State Fair of Texas, and already men are on the sidewalks, beefy men with the broad shoulders of bail bondsmen, holding up crude signs fashioned out of brown cardboard and lettered in black shoe polish. "Need 2 Tickets." To what? The Ice Capades?

An ocean of humanity is marching toward the fairgrounds, advancing from all directions. The night before, the Dallas cops had arrested 471 celebrants on downtown streets. Police reported that the size of the Friday mob had been smaller than the previous year's, but seemed more wasted. One of the Dallas newspapers ran a front-page photo of a man in handcuffs, wearing a court jester's hat. He had the exact same expression on his face that Jack Nicholson wore in that "Here's Johnny!" scene when he hacks through the door in *The Shining*. The paper also carried a front-page box score from the annual Friday Night Fiasco, the two "teams" being Texas-OU Revelers versus Cops that included stat categories like "Fines: Revelers $12,292, Cops 0" and "Police Cars Lost: Revelers 0, Cops 2."

People had been hanging out of every window on every floor at the Adolphus and the Baker hotels, gawking at the bipolar jamboree taking place on the sidewalks of Commerce Street beneath, too enthralled with this pageant of madness to heave down any furniture. The incidence of what the police call "debris droppage" had been low this year, thank God. A temporary fence, barbed wire, had been erected by the police around an empty lot next door to the Baker. Tents were set up within, which were actually rustic little outdoor holding tanks for the arrestees, before they were transported away in the paddy wagons. How barbaric. Somehow it is difficult to imagine a stockade such as that being constructed to cope with the low jinks associated with perhaps the Brown-Colgate game.

The constabulary, its ranks of *six hundred* outnumbered on the ground by this ten-thousand-man army of the impaired, had seemed well in control. Then, around 10:30, after the high school games were over, another tidal surge of high-beam highlights and blaring horns came gushing into the concrete caverns of Lunatic City, and the dipsomaniacal frenzy throbbed on past midnight. At last, in an annual downtown Dallas tradition far more spectacular and entertaining than the Neiman Marcus Christmas parade, the fire engines began to rumble slowly along Commerce, literally blasting the remaining celebrants off their feet and off the sidewalk. This was the Dallas Fire Department's subtle reminder that it was time to go on home.

That was Friday, though, and now it's game day, and the foreplay is over. Now the bus has been waved through the east end of the fairground, past the massive old steam locomotives they keep on display, and on toward the stadium. The Texas-OU fans are easily distinguishable from the remainder of the enormous fairgoing multitudes, and not just because of the orange-

and-crimson attire. They're bug-eyed; their faces are ablaze with lavish expectations.

Imagine, then, what is going on in the pit of Mike Cotten's stomach as the starting quarterback for the favored Texas Longhorns gazes, expressionless, from the window of the bus as it creeps past the livestock barns and rodeo area and nears the south end of the Cotton Bowl, where locker rooms of both teams are situated. Cotten, kind of thick legged and no taller than five-foot-ten, was anything but the prototypical NFL quarterback, every bit the Darrell Royal prototype. Steady. Never turned the ball over and would put it in the air only in the case of a national emergency.

Composure under combat extremes, that's what's required to play quarterback amid the cannon fire on the stadium floor at the Texas-Oklahoma game. And Mike Cotten, because of the ferocious tension out there, knows that in this particular game the stress factor is quick to expose a mistake-prone offense. "I think . . . this might be a tough one today," says the UT quarterback, sipping on a gin fizz as the bus finally arrives at the stadium. That's number three for Mike, by the way, and it's still an hour before kickoff. Even at that, Cotten is probably more sober than the other occupants of the bus, except perhaps the driver, and some are drinking vodka and champagne right out of the bottle, taking one last pull, before steadying themselves, climbing down, and heading into the stadium.

I should perhaps clarify here that this is happening at the beginning of the 1971 game. Mike Cotten actually started the *1961* game, and no, this wasn't the Longhorns' team bus. It was chartered by a Highland Park guy who was throwing a big party at his house the morning before the game, and Cotten had been one of the guests. Texas won that 1961 game, 28–7, the season that Royal introduced the flip-flop offense, where they lined up strong side, weak side on every play instead of right side, left side, the way it had been conventionally done. That flip-flop worked great in 1961, but it had a lot to do with the tailback, James Saxton. Royal described Saxton's running style as "what happens when you blow up a balloon and turn it loose." He wound up high in the voting for the Heisman Trophy that Ernie Davis wound up winning, and after Saxton graduated, the flip-flop was never as effective. Now all of that seemed archaic compared to the scorched-earth exhibitions from the Wishbone T.

The 1971 game would be the fourth installment of Royal's Wishbone era in Dallas, and the Sooners hadn't been able to slow it down in the previous three. Not the Sooners or any-one else, until Ara Parseghian and Notre Dame had broken the Horns' thirty-game winning streak the previous New Year's Day in the Cotton Bowl game. Texas had fumbled the ball all over the field that afternoon, though, and now the Longhorns were back in Dallas on the same artificial turf, a playing surface that favored the swift, and they were dead-set for atonement.

Steve Worster, the storming bull of a fullback and the real diesel engine of the Wishbone ever since Royal had cranked the thing up in 1968, was gone. Jim Bertelsen, a halfback good enough to play for the L.A. Rams, was back, though. So people figured that if the 1971 version of the Longhorns was due for a slowdown, it wouldn't be much of one.

I was in Austin for media day before the '71 season, and Royal seemed unusually upbeat. "Our offense," he said, "will be another good one." Huh. That wasn't exactly Ali predicting that Sonny Liston or somebody would "hit the floor in Round Four" or some damn thing. Still, that assessment, with people in the lineup who'd never played, was almost cocky by Royal's standards. But Royal loved his quarterback, Eddie Phillips.

Royal told this story about going wolf hunting in a helicopter in Mexico the previous spring. (When you coach the Longhorns football team, you get invited to all kinds of outdoor adventures like that.) "This wolf was moving in on a little herd of sheep, but then the helicopter carrying the guys with the rifles flew over the ridge, and boy, all of a sudden, the game changed," Royal said "Same deal, sort of, in a scrimmage the other day. The defense was beating the hell out of the offense. And then I put Eddie back out there."

The Longhorns' retooled 1971 model of the Wishbone *was* a good one, too, rolling nicely in an opening win over UCLA in the Coliseum. Then Phillips hurt a hamstring. Backup Donnie Wigginton quarterbacked the Horns to easy wins over Texas Tech and an Oregon Ducks team that included Dan Fouts. But gawd a'mighty, Wigginton was only five-foot-eight, and now Royal was facing OU and having to do without that helicopter and its crew of onboard snipers. On Wednesday before the Saturday game, Phillips said that he was gimping along a hallway in a dorm when he'd felt something "pop," and all of a sudden the sore leg no longer hurt. Phillips swung the leg around and he was healed. Maybe an act of providence, although the team doctor figured perhaps some scar tissue had broken loose.

So Eddie Phillips practiced on Wednesday, and on Thursday morning, his leg felt worse than ever. Royal announced that Wigginton would be his man against the Sooners, and mustered whatever confidence he could because there was something unsettling about taking on the bitterest of rivals with a quarterback whom everybody calls Little Donnie.

Meanwhile, the quarterback for the Sooners, Jack Mildren, had been a genuine bright-light headliner of the Texas high school football star system. After winning the most hotly contested recruiting competition for any Texas high schooler in the entire decade of the 1960s, the effort to land Mildren was finally reaching fruition.

I'd seen Mildren's final high school game, the AAAA state finals. Mildren played at Cooper High in Abilene and was a rollout whiz. Coming into the championship game, he had been theretofore unstoppable. The championship game was at a neutral site, the TCU stadium in Fort Worth, against Reagan High from Austin. I'd called the Reagan coach for his comments for a pregame interview, and he climbed my ass pretty badly and was pissed because all of Fort Worth was pouring praise all over Jack Mildren and not giving his team a trace of a chance. "Who died and made Jack Mildren God?" said the coach, Travis Raven. I thought Raven was a prick and was pulling like hell for Mildren and his Cooper team. Mildren's coach, Merrill Green, had played for Bud Wilkinson and made an eighty-yard run that helped the Sooners beat Texas in 1953.

That high school championship game was played in the closest thing that Texas has to offer to a blizzard. Freezing rain and sleet. Fierce north wind. The sportswriters sat huddled in the press box, high, high, above the field, sipping scotch out of paper cups. Ben Hogan was up there, too. Hogan was a huge football fan and had come to see Jack Mildren, like everyone else. Hogan had been allowed in the warmth of the press box because, well, he was Ben Hogan. The game turned out to be a Texas high school football classic, almost eerily similar to the Dallas–Green Bay Ice Bowl game that was going to be played in a couple of weeks.

Like the Packers in the Ice Bowl, Mildren's team, highly favored, was behind. Reagan, north wind to its back, had rallied with a fourth-quarter TD and led, 20–19. Now Mildren, like Bart Starr had done, directed the final drive, firing a couple of fourth-down completions to sustain the march, with sleet blowing right into his face. With the clock running off the final few seconds, Abilene Cooper, now at the Austin Reagan one-yard line with no time-outs, eschewed the chip-shot field goal. Like Bart Starr, Jack Mildren ran a quarterback sneak, and unlike Bart Starr, his feet slid from underneath him, and he didn't get in. So the clock ran out, and Cooper lost. That hardly would tarnish Jack Mildren's image as the schoolboy par excellence and the all-American boy. Every college in the United States was offering Jack everything but three wishes if he'd only come to its campus and partake of its marvelous academic resources.

Finally Mildren culled the list to two candidates. Oklahoma and SMU, which, according to various former students, stands for Suck Me Unconscious. The Dallas-based Mustangs scarcely enjoyed the football heritage of the Oklahoma Sooners. With alumni such as Lamar Hunt, owner of the Kansas City Chiefs, working hard to sway Mildren to Big D, the Ponies could present an impressive portfolio of persuasive little perks. The Ponies, when they wanted to, knew how to get their man and had beaten out the Sooners for the top recruit in the United States a decade previous—Glynn Gregory, also from Abilene.

This time, the Sooners, under first-year coach Chuck Fairbanks, sealed the deal. Not only did OU obtain the services of a premier quarterback, the state of Oklahoma additionally secured the services of an excellent new director of parks administration in the form of Jack Mildren's dad, Larry.

Now, four years later, the recruiting effort to entice Mildren to Sooner-ville was paying serious dividends. The Sooners' version of the Wishbone, an effort that had some fits and starts when Fairbanks installed the offense the season before, was developing into what the crimson-and-cream loyalists realized was a sight to behold. Mildren was joined in Fairbanks's Wishbone by two other Texans at halfback, Greg Pruitt from Galveston and long-striding Joe Wiley from the sticks of East Texas in Henderson. Wiley ran the 120-yard high hurdles in 13.8. He could flat fly, and Pruitt was even faster.

I had been unable to interview Darrell Royal for some pre-game stories I had prepared for the *Fort Worth Press* that week. This was OU week, after all, and Royal had other things on his mind than chitchat with pissant sportswriters. Or at least, the ones in Fort Worth. People on the UT coaching staff said Royal became a different sort of person during preparations for the annual Sooner challenge. Line coach Willie Zapalac said that "you can just feel it, when he walks into the office early on Monday morning."

I did speak on the phone with another of the UT assis-tants, Bill Ellington, who said that Royal described his oppo-nent as "the best OU team I've seen in my fifteen years here [at Texas]."

"And I concur," Ellington said. "You can run down a check-list pertaining to football, and you'd have to rate Oklahoma as good or excellent in every category. I am talking about every phase, including the kickoff game. They kick it out of the end zone every play. Turn it around and they have excellent kick men. Look at that OU offense. Everything is there. A deep threat. An inside threat. An outside threat to both sides."

"Can they throw?" I asked him, already knowing the answer. I'd seen Mildren move his high school team on that drive against the wind in the sleet, and I knew damn well he could throw. Bill Ellington provided a good response. "Throw? Hell, when it's second-and-one every time, you don't need to throw."

The Sooners beat SMU 30–0 in rain in the season opener, showing the Ponies what they had missed out on in Jack

Mildren. An SMU assistant coach told me off the record that "if it had been on a dry field, Oklahoma would have beaten us a zillion to nothing instead of thirty to nothing." Then the Sooners steamrolled Pittsburgh 55–29, and after that they opened the eyes of the nation by beating the USC Trojans team, featuring Sam Cunningham and Lynn Swann, 33–20. Greg Pruitt ran for 216 yards against USC, and afterward, John McKay, the sharp-tongued Trojan coach and master of West Coast college football, marveled that "all we could do was stand there and watch Oklahoma run past us." McKay was the coach who, after he left USC to coach the Tampa Bay Bucs, was asked what he thought about his team's execution after a bad loss, and he said, "I'd be in favor of it."

And after his encounter with the blazing Sooners offense, McKay conceded, "We did do a good job of tackling the Oklahoma fullback—on the plays when he didn't have the ball."

McKay offered a prediction on the upcoming Texas-OU outcome. "This is a classic example of the immovable object meeting the irresistible force. Oklahoma feels they can't be stopped. Texas feels they can't be stopped, or so it seems. So I think the score should be 500 to 500—at the end of the first quarter."

Bill Ellington went on and on about that Sooners backfield. "Their overall speed is just fantastic. I don't know how fast Greg Pruitt is, but he outran a pretty good man in the USC game. Alonzo Thomas ran the opening leg on USC's sprint relay team that won the NCAA championship, and I watched Thomas on film. At the start of a play, he's chasing Pruitt, and at the end of the run, he's still chasing him."

The Longhorns were favored by five and a half points on the morning of the game, but that margin was based mostly on

Texas's performances that were a little too much in the past. So far that year, the UT offense hadn't looked as swift and deadly as during the three previous seasons.

I took my seat in the jammed Cotton Bowl press box knowing two things: One, my editor back at the *Fort Worth Press* was furious with me. He complained about the sports section running too many photos of black players. In response, I designed the sports section of the Friday edition to include the photos of twenty-three athletes, all of them black. (Boy, he *was* pissed off, too, but a couple of weeks later, the reporter that the *Press* sent to cover the TCU-Baylor game in Waco filed a story that said the Frogs had finally won a game, midway through the season, under new coach Jim Pittman. What the story failed to point out was that during the second quarter of the Baylor game, Pittman had dropped dead on the sideline. So after that, I didn't look so bad.)

And two, as the teams ran onto the field while the stadium seemed to quake, I knew that Oklahoma was going to beat Texas, and I regretted not having wagered my car payment on the Sooners, taking those five and a half points.

What I had not anticipated was the fashion in which the Sooners dominated the afternoon. This was not simply a win over the Texas Longhorns, huge as that was. What Mildren, Pruitt, Wiley, and a galaxy of other Sooners did was establish a New Day for Oklahoma football, and the swashbuckling Sooners and their signature running attack—swift, elusive, rampaging, brilliant—wouldn't slow down for another sixteen seasons. The stars of the unforgettable Oklahoma team on that October Saturday would, through the coming seasons, be replaced by a roll call of the greats—Joe Washington, Billy Sims, Kenny King. Yet no Sooners, past or future, would produce a more devastating performance than that display Greg Pruitt put on against the Longhorns.

Pruitt, a jet in cleats, danced and juked all around the Cotton Bowl AstroTurf. After he'd made all the Longhorn defenders trip over themselves and fall down like drunks trying to ice skate, he'd downshift and accelerate like an AA fuel dragster, and all the Longhorns could do was stand there and wave good-bye. Not only to Greg Pruitt, but to any hopes of beating OU for the next six years. One sportswriter would claim that, against the Longhorns, Pruitt resembled a man riding an invisible motorcycle.

I wrote that Chuck Fairbanks unveiled the offense of the future: the Whoosh-Bone T. Coming into the OU game, the most rushing yards that Texas had surrendered in team history were 310 by Texas Tech in 1967. Against the '71 Longhorns, the Sooners had surpassed that number by halftime. The Longhorns, in truth, were playing their guts out. They'd scored first, behind the backup QB Wigginton, after Pruitt fumbled early. Then—zap—Pruitt raced forty-six yards to the Texas two-yard line and scored himself two plays later. Texas issued a brave counterpunch. Bobby Callison, the fullback replacing the departed and sorely missed Steve Worster, ran for thirteen yards, then seventeen more, and Wigginton the backup QB ran forty-four yards for the go-ahead TD.

The Sooners, wearing white jerseys, came back with ridiculous ease. Mildren ran the keeper five yards upfield, then pitched late to the trailing Pruitt, who continued upfield for twenty yards more. "That's the Wishbone play," Pruitt would comment afterward, describing the issue in terms the neophyte could understand. "When Jack gets out there, he makes the defensive backs come up to him, and when he can't go anymore, he pitches it to me, and I take off."

"They're like water moving across downhill land, and when they get outside, they scald the corners," was the way Royal described the scene as he watched it from the sideline on the west side of the Cotton Bowl. So the Sooners tied the game, 14–14, and scored again to take the lead for good on a ninety-six-yard drive that averaged just about a first down per play. Now up by a touchdown, the Sooners stormed back again, while the Texas defense was scratching, clawing, and clinging to the little branch on the cliffside. OU was approaching the Texas end zone again, and if they got in, the Longhorns could stop playing "Texas Fight" and switch to "Taps." Darrell Royal had said that for a head coach to be successful, he had to "dig, wheedle, and coax that fanatical effort out of the players. You want them to play every Saturday like they were planting the flag on Iwo Jima." Royal was seeing that effort now. But defeating the Japanese was one thing; stopping this Oklahoma whirlwind seemed the more daunting proposition. A holding call against the Sooners provided the Horns with some apparent relief, as the ball was moved back to the UT twenty. The next play, Pruitt sliced into the UT secondary. Around the ten-yard line, Alan Lowry—a UT defensive back and a good one, all-Southwest Conference, in fact—had a clean shot at Pruitt, but then did an impersonation of a man dancing badly and without a partner, and while Lowry was doing that, Greg Pruitt had hauled ass like Dorothy leaving Kansas and spiked the ball onto the end-zone carpet.

"That move just gave me a head cold," marveled UT sports publicist Jones Ramsey, sitting in the press box. Ramsey, the man who had said that there are only two sports in Texas—football and spring football—and "the only thing more boring than track is field," was a man impossible to impress, and now he was impressed, too. The Longhorns refused to surrender. Little Donnie kept plugging away until the Sooners' Glen King—from Jacksboro, Texas, home of the Green Frog Café and OU's first black captain—slammed into the gutsy QB. Wigginton left the field on a stretcher, experiencing that lack-of-energy malaise a person feels after his or her rib cage gets yanked. The gimpy Eddie Phillips entered the game, but not the same Eddie Phillips whom Royal was describing with his helicopter-versus-the-wolf parable. What Royal was watching now was a new formation: the Wheelchair T. Phillips never regained his preinjury form, so he married Tom Landry's daughter and lived happily ever after.

Oklahoma went on to beat Texas, 48–27, and demonstrated the offensive template that would enable the Sooners to "strap a half a hundred," as Barry Switzer used to love to say, not only to the Kansas States but to virtually any other football team that would fall beneath the wheels of this new Oklahoma offensive battlewagon. The first time scientists split the atom, it was done beneath the stands of a football stadium at the University of Chicago. They weren't entirely sure that they might not blow up the world. So it was fitting and appropriate that football physicists at OU—Fairbanks and company—chose another stadium, the Cotton Bowl, in which to unleash the ultimate offensive doomsday machine. "They cut us up like boardinghouse pie, and that's real small pieces," said Darrell Royal.

After the onslaught, the Texas players seemed bewildered. The locker room contained an assembly of proud players who knew that they'd been had. They showered and dressed while listening to the Sooner band blasting "Boomer Sooner" up through the south end of the Cotton Bowl.

"There really isn't a lot to say, is there?" was the honest assessment of Don Burrisk, a sophomore halfback who started the game for the Longhorns. "They have fantastic speed, too much speed for us today. We knew they could beat us outside. And they did. That Pruitt is unbelievable."

Stan Mauldin, a Texas linebacker and defensive mainstay on most days—but not this day—attempted to describe his experience against the Oklahoma Sooners. "Greg Pruitt is so fast that he's hard to see," Mauldin said.

Chuck Fairbanks wore the relieved expression of a man who had just passed a roadside Breathalyzer test. Just a year earlier, he had been attempting to explain to the impatient OU fans, via the media, why his version of the Texas Wishbone was a work in progress after being plowed beneath the Cotton Bowl's synthetic playing field, to the tune of 41–9.

"My decision to go to the Wishbone looks a lot better than it did a year ago," Fairbanks opined. He could afford an excursion into understatement, realizing that throughout the Sooner State, thousands of fans were at work scraping those "Chuck Chuck" stickers off their back bumpers.

That Saturday night, late, I got a phone call from a voice from the past. It was Joe Don, and years after being expelled from the football ranks in Norman, he said, "How about OU?" He'd watched the game from a farmhouse on some deep rural land in East Texas that his father owned. "If we'd had Mildren and Pruitt, we'd have walked all over Texas." Memories of '63. Looney had gotten shipped off to Vietnam because of his full-scale exposure to, well, dope and guns. He'd kind of hated to leave. It was the Texas game that kept on giving him nightmares.

So I drove out to see Joe Don at the farm three weeks later, figuring he was lonesome in the isolation of the deep woods. However, a slender brunette woman was leaving the farmhouse as I arrived. She was a student at Longview High School but could have passed for twenty-one. There was a lot of incense burning inside the house. Other than the fact that Looney had lost about a hundred pounds since I'd last seen him, he hadn't changed a bit. Well, some. His belief system was restructured into the whole Eastern culture thing, carried to the vastest extreme. Looney was now into yoga and could do a one-handed headstand while turning the rest of his body into a granny knot. Levitation was going to be his next trick. The power of the mind can conquer anything. That's how he'd lost the weight, by fasting for forty-three days, mostly on water and lemon juice. Now all that was left of Looney was flesh, bones, and veins. He looked like a Martian and spent the idle hours firing off his Vietnam-souvenir machine gun out in the pasture, which later became a well-publicized mistake.

"There are people in Asia who can kind of de-atomize themselves, vanish, walk through walls," he insisted. I thought that was the most outlandish bunch of crap I'd ever heard, and still did until I watched the Trojans of Southern Cal try to tackle Vince Young.

In the November of one of Barry Switzer's lesser campaigns, in 1983, I got a call in Dallas from Looney. He was back in North America for the first time in eight years. By then, Looney had become a spiritual follower of the Swami Muktananda, or Baba, as he was known to his inner circle. Joe Don moved to India, then traveled the world with Baba, working as his bodyguard. Looney remembered accompanying Baba to visit the swami's swami, a man Looney called Ziparana, the ultimate master. "Ziparana was living in a barnyard, sitting naked on top of a pile of cow shit," he said, savoring the adventure. "He said, 'Hey, Baba, you got any rupees? Throw them on the ground.' So Baba tossed out some cash and said, 'See? Even the pigs won't touch it.'"

Baba died suddenly. Looney hightailed it back to the States. He was sitting in an airport in Indonesia, mourning Baba, when he decided to do something novel. He got drunk. "I drank about twelve beers, and then I turned to some guy at the bar and said, 'Money and pussy. That's all that matters.'"

But in the fall of '83, Looney's life took on an added fixation: football. He'd returned to the farm in East Texas, where he had his pyramid and where he'd been busted by the feds for possession of his machine gun. Daingerfield, Texas, was not far along the blacktop from Looney's farm, and the Daingerfield Tigers, playing AAA ball, had outscored their opponents six hundred and sixty something to six. Looney was following Daingerfield into Fort Worth for a playoff game against Post, a town named after the same Post of Toasties fame. He had actually been attending Tigers workouts, chatting it up with some of the players.

Did they know anything about his football background? "They don't know me from Adam," Looney said.

Daingerfield slaughtered Post, with Looney in the stands yelling his guts out. After the game, he watched as one of the Daingerfield players argued with a cheerleader. Then she slapped the crap out of him. "God, does that bring back the memories," Looney said.

The next time I saw Joe Don, he was lying in a casket in a funeral home in Alpine, Texas. If you're looking for remote and spiritual, Alpine's your place. Looney had bought land out there and built a dome house, surrounded by some fruit and vegetable orchards and a windmill-powered irrigation system. Joe Don had it all together. On a September Saturday, he was riding his motorcycle to meet a friend for a bike tour of Big Bend National Park. Looney missed an S-curve. His bike left the road, Looney's neck was broken, and he died on the spot.

At age forty-six, Looney died the way nineteen-year-olds are supposed to. Looney's father, Don, sobbed all through the funeral service. A smattering of teammates from Cameron were there, not many. Alpine is a hard place to get to, though.

The women's basketball team from Sul Ross State University served as honorary pallbearers.

Wherever he went, Joe Don really knew how to make friends.

9

Feeding the Monster

Nobody has contributed more to the enrichment of the Texas and Oklahoma game than the unrestrainable Barry Switzer, damned as a "sorry bastard" by Darrell Royal and eventually forced to leave when the public perception of the OU program was that of a yard scene at Alcatraz. Switzer's sixteen-year tenure as head coach saw an era of breathtaking gridiron dynamics.

Switzer's football team reflected his personal style. Bold. All systems go. Screw the countdown, let's blast off now. After Chuck Fairbanks abruptly departed Norman following the 1972 season to go coach the New England Patriots, Switzer was elevated to the pilot's seat. Switzer was thirty-five.

His assumption of command at (arguably, but not too much so) the premier program in college football capped a remarkable life ascendency for the boy from the wrong side of the tracks, in a part of the world where the right side of the tracks was scary, too. As a kid in Arkansas, Switzer would wade into the swamps where they now find giant prehistoric woodpeckers and pull fish out of the water that were even weirder than the bird life. It remains doubtful that Barry caught any fish, though, that were as strange as the human kind that surrounded him. When Switzer was a teenager, his mother shot herself to death while he was in the house. His dad, Frank, served time after being charged with a variety of indiscretions, primarily selling bootleg booze and heaven knows what else to the backwoods secular set.

Switzer discovered solace in life in the form of football . . . and solace would transform into nirvana when the Oklahoma head-coaching post was placed in his hands.

He was ecstatic that he had been selected for the job, having thought that the Sooners might try to hire Royal, as they'd done twice during the 1960s. Royal was staying put in Austin. So Switzer was the man. He understood the job requirements with crystal clarity. "I didn't create the monster," Switzer said. "George Cross and Bud Wilkinson did that. My job is to feed the monster."

Switzer loved to court thoroughbreds, as the ultimate players' coach, and groom them to become stars. Oklahoma Sooners fans might remember some of them. Lucius Selmon. Eddie Foster. Randy Hughes. John Roush. Joe Washington. Rod Shoate. Tinker Owens. Jimbo Elrod. Billy Brooks. Mike Vaughn. Terry Webb. Dewey Selmon. Lee Roy Selmon. Zac Henderson. Greg Roberts. Daryl Hunt. Reggie Kinlaw. Billy Sims. George Cumby. Terry Crouch. Ricky Bryan. Kevin Murphy. Tony Casillas. Darrell Reed. Keith Jackson. Dante Jones. Rickey Dixon. Mark Hutson. Anthony Phillips. Each one, somebody's selection as a first-team all-American while Switzer reigned in Norman.

That roster of names represents every position except quarterback. If all-American honors were bestowed on the basis of wings rather than forward passing statistics, Switzer would have had about four of those as well. Still, Barry Switzer would become the only coach in college history to have players win the Heisman, Outland, Lombardi, Butkus, and Thorpe awards.

The Switzer star system spawned football teams that worked the land with the fury of a category five twister. Three times—1974, 1975, 1985—Switzer's Sooners won national championships. With the Orange Bowl game being the Sooners' ultimate postseason destination (the Big Eight champion automatically went to Miami on New Year's), Switzer's teams hit South Florida with the frequency of tropical storms. OU, despite having to overcome Nebraska's Big Red Cornhusker Machine to get there, traveled to Miami four straight years under Switzer—twice. His .821 winning percentage at Norman is the fourth best in national history, and there was not a coach of renown in Switzer's time—Royal, Tom Osborne, Woody Hayes, Joe Paterno, Jimmy Johnson—whom Switzer didn't beat. The unrelenting success of his program during Switzer's prime years in Norman prompted the OU president, Bill Banowsky, to make his memorable comment about his mission to build a university "that the entire football team will be proud of."

Switzer knew how to recruit. He was proud of his ability to convincingly sweet-talk the offspring of some of his father's best clients. Switzer knew how to party. Until Mike Price came along in his remarkably abbreviated career at Alabama, no coach in college football partied more flamboyantly than Barry. His enthusiasms conformed nicely to the Tom T. Hall song about faster horses, older whiskey, and younger women. After Barry's wife gave him an unconditional release in 1981, he undertook his pursuit of the latter with gusto. If Switzer gave a damn about what anybody thought of that, including the college president, he certainly didn't allow that concern to interfere with his activities in the social sector.

"Barry," says one OU grad, fan, season-ticket holder, and heavy contributor to the athletic fund, "had what people nowadays might refer to as libido issues. If there was a pretty woman in the room, Barry would hit on her. She could be sitting there with her husband—didn't matter if it was a senator's wife—and Barry would make his move. If anybody had a problem with that, Barry sure as hell didn't regard it as *his* problem."

Switzer's choice of social companions eventually caused concerns with the appearance-of-impropriety zealots within the OU administration. Toward the end of his tenure, acting OU president David Swank came at Barry with a big tut-tut. Somebody claimed to have seen Switzer in a hotel suite in Las Vegas where some people were allegedly sucking Peruvian marching powder up their noses. Switzer was indignant. Later, Switzer would reflect, "Well, it might have been true. I don't know. You could walk into any saloon or boardroom at any time, particularly seven or eight years ago, and cocaine might be present. What was I supposed to do, shout, 'Here comes Barry Switzer! Hide your dope!' every place I went?"

Switzer could have solved that dilemma by simply avoiding saloons and boardrooms. Whatever. Barry Switzer's fondness for mingling with the show ponies remains a distant postscript to the fabulous imprint he would leave forever on the Oklahoma Sooner football heritage. Sure, he could recruit, coach, and pursue the enjoyment of life with hedonistic zeal, but what Switzer knew how to do best was beat the hell out of Texas, and he did it so convincingly that Darrell Royal was driven to an early retirement.

The day Switzer accepted the role of head coach and supreme commander of Sooners football, he understood at once that the October date in Dallas was the one that would determine the length of his Norman tenure.

"The way to keep OU fans happy is simply beat Texas," Switzer said. "Sure, coaches will say that's just one of many games. But that's just bullshit. That Red River rumble is *the* game. Part of it is the old Okie inferiority complex. The Dust

Bowl business. That's something that everybody in this state feels at one time or another. There's no better cure for that than kicking Texas's butt.

"Another factor is that so many OU grads live in enemy territory. I don't think a Texas grad has ever come north of the Red River to make a living, but a lot of OU grads have gone south."

Barry Switzer—college football's leading proponent of the Big Bang theory—made his Dallas debut with a detonation that echoed across both states. The game was a rout. OU buried the Longhorns, 52–13—the worst loss in Darrell Royal's coaching term in Austin. UT—finally—had a black star, fullback Roosevelt Leaks, who would return to Dallas three weeks later and set a Southwest Conference single-game rushing record—342 yards—against SMU. But Leaks wasn't a factor against OU. Nobody wearing an orange jersey would be. The day belonged to Joe Washington and his backfield kinsmen at Oklahoma as they poured through the UT defense for more than 500 yards total offense. Afterward, Royal said, "After a defeat like that, all you can say is that you got beat by a vastly superior football team."

As that continued to occur, however, Royal's postgame remarks would gradually drift off from the conventional head coach protocols of quotesmanship. A grudge factor—Royal versus Switzer—was developing, and it became something that would finally engulf the great UT coach.

Switzer, to the everlasting elation of the Oklahoma fans, turned up the heat in the Cotton Bowl. The 1974 game was closer than the oddsmakers had figured—a helluva lot closer than the '73 ass-battering that the Sooners had inflicted on Texas—but the Sooners came through at the end, 16–13, and Switzer learned then that the close-shave wins in Dallas would feel even more gratifying than the blowouts.

Texas put together a team in 1975 that Royal thought was

capable of finally beating the Sooners. Marty Akins had developed into a whizbang Wishbone quarterback. The contest became a back-and-forth barn burner. By now, my media job situation was taking me to the World Series rather than the Texas-OU game. So—during the opening game of the greatest World Series ever played, between Cincinnati and Boston—I would periodically check the AP teletype machine in the Fenway Park press-box to check on the progress of the football game in Dallas. Actually, I only checked twice. First time, Texas had just kicked a field goal to tie the game at seventeen. The second time, the teletype reported that Horace Ivory, an Oklahoma halfback from a Catholic high school in Fort Worth, had run thirty-seven yards for a fourth-quarter touchdown, and Oklahoma won the game, 24–17, en route to another national championship.

In Austin, the mood was getting ugly. Royal had begun insisting that the Switzer regime was working by its own rules—not the NCAA's—when it came down to the definition of "improper" in recruiting top high school football talent, particularly the talent in the state of Texas. Switzer said he couldn't understand why *Royal* couldn't understand that OU's winning climate was sufficient to attract the Lone Star talent to drift northward and that no financial incentives were necessary. Royal demurred. One player who did evade the Sooners recruiting net, a halfback from Fort Worth, Ivey Suber, went to Texas. Royal made it public that Suber's mother had told him that Switzer had visited her home and offered her son a new wardrobe, a new Pontiac, and a grand in walking money if he'd come to Oklahoma. Switzer used his favorite word, *bullshit,* to refute the allegation. What Switzer did confirm was that he had visited Suber in the locker room of his Fort Worth high school and told the prospect that if he committed to the Longhorns, he'd better get used to looking at a lot of white faces in the UT offensive huddle.

The animosity reached declaration-of-war magnitude as the 1976 game approached. In fact, the temperatures in Darrell Royal's football kitchen had reached such an intensity that bacon grease was spattering out of UT's skillet. New allegations from Austin were that OU had hired an operative to spy on Longhorn workouts. So Royal issued an unprecedented challenge: He dared Switzer and other members of his staff to take a lie-detector test and answer questions concerning the spying charges. If the Sooners passed the polygraph, Royal would pay $10,000 to the coach's favorite charity. Switzer quickly declined Royal's generous offer, saying that it was worth more to him to watch the UT coach consume himself with "chasing ghosts." (Switzer would later agree that Royal was right about the spying charges, adding that "when Richard Nixon did the same thing I did, they called it Watergate.")

The pregame festivities in 1976 became awkward. Gerald Ford, now president of the United States and seeking a contract renewal from the voters of Texas and Oklahoma, attended the game to toss the coin. Switzer, Royal, and the president stood at the mouth of the Cotton Bowl tunnel. The two coaches were no longer on speaking terms and were attempting small talk with Gerald Ford when a drunk Oklahoma fan shouted, "Hey! Who are those two assholes with Switzer?"

Royal's team, and it was a particularly good one, battled the Sooners with as much heart and zeal as any he would bring to Dallas. The contest was ruled by brutal defense, and every yard gained by either team would come at the expense of a pickup-truck tankful of sweat, blood, and snot. Texas, with two field goals, seemed on the verge of making that stand up. With UT leading 6–0 and the clock winding inside the final five minutes, Ivey Suber, the object of the earlier recruiting controversy, sloppily hit the OU line carrying the football in his left arm. The ball popped loose, OU recovered inside Texas territory and scored what appeared to be the winning touchdown with just a minute and a half to play.

Then—just before the formality of kicking the winning extra point—UT linebacker Lionel Johnson leaned across from Sooners center Kevin Craig and said, "Hey, center. I bet you snap it over his head. Bet you snap it over his head." Oh, the power of suggestion. After the botched snap, Bud Hebert, the holder, retrieved the ball and passed it into the end zone, but UT picked it off. The resulting 6–6 conclusion was the most distasteful outcome for both teams perhaps in the history of the series and would maintain that ranking until 1984, when the same thing happened again.

Afterward, Royal trudged from the field and up the Cotton Bowl tunnel for the final time. At age fifty-two, he retired from coaching at the conclusion of the season. Royal—the ultimate "plow the straight row" kind of guy—would devote the remainder of his years to a "hit the straight drive" ethic and go about the task of attempting to shoot his age on the golf course. When he wasn't swinging the golf club, Royal was spending time with various noted pickers and grinners from the Austin music scene.

Barry Switzer was quick to applaud Royal for his decision to quit coaching at a time that many of the ink-stained critics from the sports sections of the region, and many Texas fans, thought premature. For a coaching legend, he was not leaving on top. Switzer felt otherwise. "Who in his right mind wouldn't rather hang out with Willie Nelson than spend all his time in some potential recruit's living room while his dog hunches your leg?" he said.

So, while Barry Switzer would not have Darrell Royal to kick around anymore, he would have to contend against a particularly troublesome remnant of Royal's coaching regime.

William Wayne Justice, a U.S. district judge in East Texas

Fresh from the laboratory Darrell Royal unveils the plans for his "ultimate weapon." The Longhorns' Wishbone T offense cranked up to full efficiency in the 1968 Oklahoma game and proved unstoppable for the next two and a half seasons. (© Corbis)

When Michigan State coach Duffy Daugherty called Darrell Royal to inquire about his new Wishbone offense, Royal said, "You don't want my playbook, Duffy. You want my fullback." Steve Worster, the battering ram, pounds out yardage against Oklahoma in UT's come-from-behind win in 1969. (Courtesy of the University of Texas Sports Photography Department)

When you're unbeaten as a Texas quarterback, even former U.S. presidents come to pay homage. James Street, Darrell Royal, and Lyndon Baines Johnson are shown after Texas beat Notre Dame on New Year's Day, 1970. *(© Corbis)*

The ultimate players' coach, party-loving Barry Switzer enjoys his "home away from home," which was Miami and the Orange Bowl game during his golden years at OU. He revels in the scene with defensive greats and brothers Lee Roy (*left*) and Dewey Selmon. *(© Corbis)*

LEFT: Coach Darrell Royal said, "When Earl Campbell ran the ball, snot flew." Campbell rumbles for yardage against Oklahoma in his freshman season in 1974, and he wouldn't stop until he finally beat the Sooners in 1977. He won the Heisman Trophy in the process. *(Courtesy of the University of Texas Sports Photography Department)*

RIGHT: Coach Fred Akers had a tough act to follow when he replaced Darrell Royal as the UT coach in 1977. Akers seemed up to the challenge and beat Oklahoma in his first try. But he failed to beat the Sooners in his last four attempts, and that cost Akers his job. *(Courtesy of the University of Texas Sports Photography Department)*

Although quarterback Peter Gardere (#10) enjoyed a proficient career at Texas, he was hardly a world-beater—except when it counted, against Oklahoma. Gardere led the Horns to four straight wins over the Sooners (1989–1992) and became the only Longhorns quarterback since Bobby Layne to go 4-0 in the annual grudge game in Dallas. *(Courtesy of the University of Texas Sports Photography Department)*

When Mack Brown was announced as the new sheriff in town in Austin, many UT fans wondered if they weren't getting Sheriff Taylor from Mayberry RFD. Eventually, they'd learn that there was more to their coach than country-boy charm. (© *Corbis*)

Appropriate game-day attire is a must for fans attending the Texas-OU sideshow. This Longhorns supporter sports a costume that tells the world that he's not from Oklahoma. (© *Corbis*)

Longhorns coach Mack Brown rallies his troops in Dallas. After five straight losses to Oklahoma, the pressure on Brown to reverse the Texas fortunes was almost overwhelming. (© *Corbis*)

Brimming with fire and desire, Oklahoma coach Bob Stoops produced five straight eye-popping wins over Texas. In the process, Stoops restored the Sooners to their accustomed position at the apex of American college football. (© *Corbis*)

Happiness is a visit to the UT end zone, as Oklahoma's Trent Smith discovers in 2002. Smith's catch gave the Sooners the lead as they beat Texas and quarterback Chris Simms, 34–24, during coach Bob Stoops's five-year mastery of Mack Brown and the Longhorns. (© *Corbis*)

Often, great Texas high school football players make even greater Oklahoma Sooners. OU running star Adrian Peterson (#28) is a sterling example. In his first appearance against Texas, Peterson ran over and through the Longhorns' defense, and he was the star of the game. (© *Corbis*)

While running back Renaldo Works finds a perfect fit for the cowboy-hat trophy that goes with winning the Texas-Oklahoma game, teammates show off their technique in flashing OU's patented upside-down Hook 'Em Horns sign as the Sooners reap the spoils of their victory in 2003. (© *Corbis*)

The ferocity of the action in the Texas-Oklahoma game usually takes a toll on freshmen quarterbacks. Here, OU's rookie QB star Rhett Bomar receives rough treatment from defensive end Tim Crowder. (© *Corbis*)

Texas players inhale the joy of the ultimate celebration—the postgame lovefest that is experienced by the winners of the October classic. After beating OU, some Longhorns fans felt that the BCS championship win at the Rose Bowl was an anticlimax. (© *Corbis*)

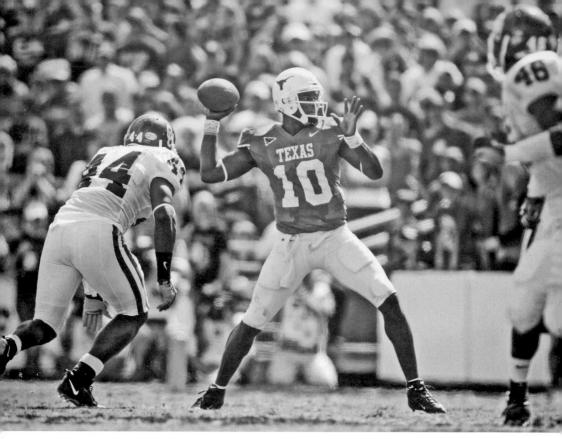

Pro scouts have labeled Vince Young's passing mechanics as "unorthodox." What was also unorthodox was Young's on-the-field results. Here, Young shreds the Oklahoma defense en route to directing Texas to a national championship. (© Corbis)

Texas defensive captain Aaron Harris ponders a new fashion trend: the silver cowboy-hat trophy that's awarded to the winner of the annual Texas-OU game. Harris was able to admire the hard hat in 2005, his fourth try after three bitter losses.
(© Corbis)

who authored sweeping mandates in the area of civil rights, was asked if he could pinpoint the one single decision in his career that made him proud, and Justice said, "Yes, it was when I made the decision to help convince Earl Campbell that the University of Texas was the best place for him."

Truly, the recruiting tug-of-war that had occurred over Campbell was as hot and frothy as East Texas had witnessed, perhaps ever. Switzer would lose out, one of the very few occasions that a premier running back from the state of Texas would elude his grasp. I had seen Campbell play against my old school, Arlington Heights, in a high school playoff quarter-finals game; I attended the contest with Joe Don Looney. The game was at Farrington Field, a high school stadium in Fort Worth, the same arena where Looney had introduced himself to the world, athletically. The stadium was packed, but nobody recognized Looney, who by then resembled a skeleton with a black ponytail that came down to his ankles. Arlington Heights had some good players, including future NFL stars Mike Renfro and Tony Franklin. Still, when Earl Campbell carried the ball for the Tyler High School Lions, he was a rhino in a petting zoo. Whether it was high school, college, or the National Football League, Campbell took on the running style of a fully loaded gravel truck, coming 'round the bend with a pilled-up driver and burned-out brakes. Watching that, I knew that if I had been athletically inclined, I would rather face a Nolan Ryan fastball, or sky-dive for that matter, than attempt to get in Campbell's way when he was en route to the nearest end zone.

After arriving at Texas, Earl Campbell would, at times, try Royal's patience in matters not entirely related to the football. After Texas had beaten the Aggies to complete Campbell's freshman season, the usual contingent of representatives of the fat-wallet club came into the UT dressing room to glad-hand the victorious troops. One such gentleman approached Campbell and introduced himself as the president of the Austin National Bank. "Goddamn, we're all sure proud to have you here in Austin," the man of finance told Campbell. "And if you're ever in the area, feel free to stop by the bank and I'll show you around."

Campbell, young and naïve, accepted the invitation under the misconception that here might be an opportunity to upgrade his automotive situation. The following Monday afternoon, Campbell presented himself in the lobby of the Austin National Bank. When he told the receptionist who he was and whom he wished to see, the woman's demeanor and body language told Campbell that perhaps he should have approached this meeting a little differently. He was, though, taken into the office of the man in charge, where Campbell was confronted by a room full of mahogany and a bank president with a mystified look on his face.

"Earl. What a surprise. What can I do for you?"

A voice inside Campbell's head was telling him now that he'd made a big mistake. Campbell gazed intently at the bank president, then said, "Do you think you could loan me five bucks?"

The bank president, at least in Campbell's view, looked stunned. He excused himself, then returned in a couple of minutes, gestured toward the telephone on his desk, and said, "Earl, would you talk to the person on line two?" The person on line two was Darrell Royal.

He said: "Earl. Have you lost your mind? Get out of there—*now*—and leave that poor man alone."

Campbell promptly complied, but that would not be the last time he would test the patience of the great coach. When Domino's Pizza opened its home-delivery operation in Austin circa 1975, Campbell and a couple of Longhorn teammates phoned in an order for sixteen large pizzas covered with everything but anchovies. When the pizzas arrived at the athletic dorm, Earl and friends accepted the pizzas, locked the deliveryman in a storage room, and enjoyed the meal. Eventually, though, Campbell and his cohorts would be summoned into Darrell Royal's office.

Campbell remembers the first words out of Royal's mouth when the meeting began: "Listen, you sons-uh-bitches . . ."

Royal would never savor the full and complete benefits of the Campbell days at Texas as a head coach. Fred Akers replaced Royal for Campbell's senior season in 1977. The Longhorns came out blazing behind their new coach. They beat Boston College 44–0, Virginia 68–0, and Rice 72–15. Was it possible that the Longhorns might have something to bring to Dallas other than a band with the world's largest drum and the usual assemblage of drunken, orange-clad fans?

By now, I wasn't covering the World Series or anything else for a Fort Worth newspaper. What I did do was visit the Dallas jail, the morning after Texas-OU Friday night, to write a feature about the annual weekend of dysfunction for an airline magazine. What I found was the saddest group of people, outside of the ones who appear in domestic relations court on child-support collections day, that you'd ever wish to encounter. In order to end their term of incarceration, the celebrants of the Friday blast were having to muster $200 cash for the drunk-and-disorderly fine, and not everybody had the dough.

"I'm glad this doesn't happen every weekend. I couldn't take it," a bailiff said.

Among the ranks of the disheartened was a twenty-year-old Oklahoman, Tom, who owned a good ticket to the game, but he despaired of his hopes of seeing the contest even though the kickoff was three hours off. Tom was out now, but the person with him when he was arrested remained locked inside the tank.

"We're waiting on a few friends," Tom said tonelessly. "We'll have to pool our resources, and I think we may have enough to get him out. But I'm afraid I am going to have to sell my ticket to be able to buy enough food and gas to get home. And"—he sighed—"I'll probably have to hire a locksmith, too. I lost my car keys when I got arrested."

That's all right, Tom. You lost your car keys? Hell. You should have seen the look on UT coach Akers's face when he lost his two quarterbacks in the first half against OU. First, the starter, Mark McBath, left with a leg injury. His replacement, John Aune, came into the game, dropped back to throw, and collapsed as if an invisible trapdoor had opened on the artificial turf beneath him. Without a Sooner putting so much as a finger on him, Aune felt his right knee give way, and he was carried off the field, his leg dangling at half mast, and his college football career was over before it had even begun.

Now Akers was down to third-string scraps. Randy McEachern, who'd never practiced with the first team and never so much as handed the ball to Earl Campbell in a workout, now was in charge of Texas's offensive destiny. He mustered one drive all day. McEachern hit wide receiver Alfred Jackson with second-quarter completions of twenty-three and eighteen yards. From the Oklahoma twenty-four yard line, Texas dispatched two receivers wide to the right side of the field. McEachern then handed the ball to Campbell on a draw play. Campbell roared through a hole at left guard, literally hurdled an OU defender at the twenty, cut past a crushing block by his tight end, Steve Hall, on OU defender Terry Peters at the ten, and barreled into the end zone. That would rank as the Texas Longhorns' run of the decade. Two monster field goals by UT's Russell Erxleben—fifty-eight and sixty-four yards—put Texas on top, 13–6. This was, though, a Barry Switzer Oklahoma team, thus fast and resourceful. With speed backs Elvis Peacock and David Overstreet looming as lethal weapons, OU quarterback Thomas Lott guided his team on a fourth-quarter drive that everyone in the stadium sensed would leave UT again deflated.

Inside five minutes to play, facing fourth and one at the Texas five-yard line, Lott ran left on the option and decided to keep the ball. UT linebacker Lance Taylor greeted Lott at the line of scrimmage. "I made a dive and bent Lott back a little," Taylor said after the game. "I was down then, looked up and saw three orange shirts on him, and they were taking him back."

The defensive stand handed Switzer his first loss in the Texas series. It was a terrific UT effort that had shut down the Sooners' attack, but Earl Campbell did them in. George Cumby, OU defensive all-American, marveled at Campbell's abilities. "Man, I hit that dude with everything I had. A lot of times, I hit with licks that should have put him out of the game. But Campbell just kept coming and coming and coming."

"This is the best Texas team we've played," announced an emotional and seemingly shell-shocked Barry Switzer.

"So how good are they?" asked a reporter.

"Well, good enough to beat Oklahoma," Switzer replied, saying all that he needed to say.

That would not be the last occasion that Switzer would sample the bitter aftertaste of a losing afternoon in Dallas. But it didn't happen often. After a 15–15 tie against Texas that happened during an absolute October monsoon—rain pouring so hard that an official evidently couldn't see an obvious interference call against a UT defender that would have won the game for the Sooners—Switzer's teams outclassed Texas. Switzer left his Oklahoma regime with a four-game winning streak against UT. He would not require any of his patented Sooner Magic to beat the Longhorns, either.

In Austin, they illuminate that tower in orange lights on the occasion of a football victory and the winning of any conference championship. So of course the orange lights weren't seen on the occasion after the 1988 season when Barry Switzer, branded man and too much bad boy, finally stepped aside in Norman. But they should have been.

10

Blood, Guts, and Corny Dogs

When the Soviet Union dissolved at the outset of the 1990s, everybody thought, "Now, that's a surprise. Well, good. Godless Commie scumbags. They had it coming, too, after the way the U.S. basketball team got screwed at the end of that Olympic game in 1972." Frankly, when you thought of the Soviet Union, the first thing that came to mind were the hairy-legged women shot-putters with the "CCCP" lettering across their sweatshirts. At least those were my sentiments.

Reactions were starkly and dramatically different when a far greater brotherhood, the Southwest Conference, decided to close shop in February 1994. The conference did not decide to disband. Rather, four members opted to move out and join with the existing Big Eight, forming what is now the Big 12. What a shocker. Unlike the Soviet Union, the Southwest Conference had a heritage and history at which it could look with pride. Other than launching their *Sputnik* and growing some barley, what did the Soviet Union ever accomplish?

The SWC, that was something else. You're talking Sammy Baugh and Doak Walker. John David Crow and Phi Slamma Jamma. What in the name of Kern Tips was going on here?

College sports fans throughout the entire state of Texas were dismayed at first. Nobody jumped from tall buildings, but untold millions bought an extra twelve-pack to help with the grieving process. It was as if they picked up the morning sports section to read that the past had been stolen. The Longhorns and Aggies and Red Raiders and Bears were invited into this new league. There, they would annually compete against Iowa State and some other schools that most Texans couldn't find on a map. And why were the Bears invited to this new show? Baylor should have been lumped among the forlorn disinherited from the old SWC . . . Houston, Rice, SMU, and TCU. Each now totally screwed.

Governor Big Hair, aka Ann Richards, was a Baylor grad. Richards was mentioned as having used her political clout to ensure that the Waco school would be included among the collegiate "haves" joining this so-called Big 12 superconference, thus ensuring the execution date for the dead old SWC. Confronted with such talk, Richards laughed and said, "That's not going to cost me any voters from my support base, because there is not a woman in the world who gives a *shit* about the Southwest Conference."

When I passed that comment along to Richards's successor in the Texas governor's mansion, George W. Bush, he laughed, too, and said, "Ann made a good point."

After the shock of learning that the SWC would close shop, the alums and fan bases of the schools cast adrift expressed the frustration and angry resentment that is always felt among the ranks of the excluded. Followers of the four schools going into the new league got philosophical in a hurry. The unraveling had been inevitable. After SMU received the NCAA death penalty for alleged serial-football-recruiting atrocities, rendering the program into a Division III–type operation, and Arkansas pulled out to join the Southeast Conference, the old SWC was doomed.

Once the tears dried and the "gone but not forgotten, at least for the next week or so" eulogies had been delivered, the reality of what loomed ahead became more sharply distinct. The Texas-OU football game now would matter even more than ever before. After all, the annual Dallas game had always been a midseason nonconference event—terrific spectacle, yes, but entirely ceremonial. The Texas-OU loser could always pick up the pieces, go out and win its conference, and play in a major bowl game. No more. Under the new Big 12 arrangement, Texas and Oklahoma were lumped into the six-team Big 12 South.

Under the new Bowl Championship Series format, the Dallas confrontation took on a more vital meaning. Unless extraordinary circumstances came into play, the loser of the Texas-OU game could still compile an eleven-win one-loss season, be listed among the top five teams in the AP poll, and still face a best-case postseason scenario of a trip to the Holiday Bowl in San Diego. If Texas and Oklahoma fielded teams that lived up to the potential offered at both programs, the Big 12 South was a two-team league. The chips on that Cotton Bowl State Fair table would henceforth be stacked twice as high.

"The dismantling of the Southwest Conference was the best thing that could have happened to the football program at the University of Texas," says Randy Rodgers. Rodgers was in charge of football recruiting at UT, under coach John Mackovic, when the school abandoned the old league. "At many conference games, the stands were pretty much empty. The bottom half of the league was not big-time college football, and if you won the Southwest Conference championship, what did you have to look forward to? A bus ride up to Dallas, to play in a freeze-your-butt-off Cotton Bowl game."

Top high school prospects throughout the state were cognizant of the declining nature of Lone Star State football—that the SWC was growing more small-time with each passing hour—

and when the invitation came to play for the Longhorns, many of the blue chips said, "Thanks, but no thanks, and I'll send you a postcard from Florida State."

With that in mind, Texas began recruiting in California, looking for the occasional seventeen-year-old who was so determined to move out of the house and out of state that he'd go anywhere, as long as it wasn't close to home. "That's how we got [eventual UT Heisman Trophy winner] Ricky Williams away from USC. Ricky just wanted to experience life outside of San Diego. He made his visit to Texas over the Christmas holidays," said Randy Rodgers. "The entire campus was deserted except for the football team, which was preparing for the Sun Bowl game against, ironically, Mack Brown's North Carolina team. Off-time to visit, but Ricky liked what he saw, and told Mackovic that he wanted to come to Texas. Mackovic didn't believe him. He said, 'We'll talk again maybe after you visit USC,' and Ricky said, 'No. I mean it. I'm coming to Texas.' Which he did, of course. But for every Ricky Williams that we'd land from out of state, six or eight of the top players in Texas would be headed elsewhere."

The decade of the 1990s had proven largely unkind to both the Texas and Oklahoma football fortunes. Mackovic had been a peculiar hire when he was chosen to replace David McWilliams as UT coach after a bad 1991 season. The Texas Longhorns program was inferior to the one at Texas A&M, so the change was not unexpected. It was just that Mackovic, who'd been the coach at Illinois, came across as being about as laid-back and local as Yasir Arafat. The word *aloof* was invented for John Mackovic, and in sessions and at fund-raising events where he was forced to rub bellies with the UT supporters, he presented all of the charm and grace of an old man's knee. He understood that and hired a public relations rep, Lisa LeMaster in Dallas, who was largely known as an image-repair specialist. A PR rival of LeMaster said, "Why doesn't she stuff his cheeks with walnuts, so he'll look cuter?" Women can be so catty.

Mackovic was not avid about the dynamics of recruiting. Defense was something that a team hired a coordinator to oversee. Mackovic was all about offense, playing golf, and sipping good wine. He once mentioned that one of his top defensive backs at UT had played high school football at "Llano Estacado." The kid must have had a swell time there, too, because Llano Estacado is not a Texas high school. It's a Texas winery. Not that Mackovic was without his moments. He beat the Texas Aggies in the final Southwest Conference game ever played. He beat Nebraska in the first-ever Big 12 championship game, too, in a huge upset. Mackovic won the game with an inspired call. On fourth down, up by three, inside three minutes to play, and needing two inches at the UT twenty-eight, Mackovic opted for a rollout pass, James Brown to tight end Derek Lewis. The play worked for sixty-one yards and won the game. Mackovic's coup was voted Play of the Year in college football and was Play of the Last Two Decades in the minds of Texas Longhorns fans. The coach was rewarded with a contract extension.

Mackovic's pedestal collapsed beneath him the following September. His empire caved in one single afternoon. Texas, ranked in the top ten, was host to UCLA and lost, 66–3. That game would rank as the most unsightly performance at home by any team in UT history. The contest grew uglier as it went along, and one monied UT backer in a stadium suite climbed onto a table and screamed, *"What's the matter with those cocksuckers?"*

Texas would limp through a 4-7 season in 1997. Based on previous performances, the Mackovic regime might have survived the troubled campaign. Mackovic, however, would encounter death by personality. His undoing occurred because when it came to the hobnobbery that is the obligation of every college head coach in the land, Mackovic did not even pretend to play. "John, through his demeanor, made it clear that he did not enjoy socializing with the rich and influential alums," says one of his former assistants at Texas. "He pretty much told those people, 'Look, I don't want to be your friend.' So—that being the case— a couple of the money people weren't at all hesitant about writing the check for the amount of John's new contract, and he was gone."

The catalytic elements that came together to bring down John Mackovic would also open the gateway to destiny for another man. The Texas coaching position was vacant and gesturing out to two candidates. One was Gary Barnett at Northwestern, who recently had grabbed the full attention of the college-coaching profession by storming to the top of the Big Ten and winning a Rose Bowl date. Jesus. If Barnett could pull that off at a piss-hole like Northwestern, imagine what he could do at Texas. Barnett was surprised that his dealings with Texas never got beyond the warm-up phase.

Tom Hicks, partner in one of the biggest investment companies in the state and owner of the Texas Rangers (the baseball team, not the cops) and the Dallas Stars NHL team, had been selected by the school to run the search team. Hicks lives in Dallas, in Highland Park really, playground of the privileged, a landscape of tree-lined streets with French-sounding names. Hicks, though, is down-home at the roots, and actually went to high school in Port Arthur with Janis Joplin. Port Arthur is home to the hardest-working people on the planet, not to mention the breeding ground for more football players of note than any town its size in the United States. The Pro Football Hall of Fame should be moved from Canton to Port Arthur. Given the natural instincts that a man such as Hicks might bring from such a place, it makes sense that he was so enamored by Mack Brown that the UT coaching quest ended the moment the two met at a hotel in Atlanta. Hicks arranged to meet Brown there at the Atlantic Coast Conference coaches meeting.

Brown came from Cookeville, Tennessee. Being from such a green and secluded Southern locale, Brown was characteristically unhurried in speech and manner. He had fashioned a winning football program at UMJ (University of Michael Jordan), not an easy thing to accomplish. Hicks deemed Brown the perfect fit for the job in Austin. DeLoss Dodds, the UT athletic director, endorsed the move. "When you move from one coach to the next in a program, there's a tendency to change some, and Gary [Barnett] and John [Mackovic], there's a lot of similarities. Mack's personality is more like Darrell Royal's. More traditional. More family-football. A Southern guy. The comfort level was there," Dodds agreed. They also couldn't help but notice that Mack Brown had been enjoying notable success in bringing top-shelf recruits to the University of North Carolina—such as defensive star Julius Peppers.

Longhorns loyalists gathered to see the new football sheriff who was coming to rescue the football team. They might have been surprised some when he turned out to be Sheriff Andy Taylor from Mayberry RFD. Brown, with his folksy delivery, seemed perhaps more fit for coaching checkers in Floyd's barbershop than football at the big plant in Texas. The people would take a wait-and-see approach to the new coach. Being from the hills, Brown at least shouldn't have been troubled by the mountain-cedar allergies that run a lot of people out of Austin.

Brown's team got off to a rocky start. The defense couldn't stop anybody. Even New Mexico State scored thirty-six points in UT's season opener. Texas was swamped again by UCLA and lost its only experienced quarterback, Richard Walton, for the season. All they had left was Major Applewhite, untested, with a barefoot-boy-with-cheeks-of-tan aura. Sheriff Taylor and Opie. What a start. But the Boys of Mayberry turned things around, upset Nebraska in Lincoln and rolled ahead from there. Then Brown showed Austin and the Big 12 why he was in Austin.

Some coaches like to control the offense. Some like to coach defense. Regard themselves as specialists. What Mack Brown specializes in is recruiting. Like all schools, Texas assigns specific regions to assistant coaches. It is their job to identify talent, ascertain which players would benefit the program, initiate the courtship process, and carry it through. Brown does things differently. Once the target high school player has been located, Brown takes over at once. And that's where he gets the jump, because, according to a person who works as a scout for several schools, "These top recruits, when it comes down to it, they don't want to talk to some goddamn assistant coach. They want to hear from the head guy."

After his 1998 opening season, Brown recruited what *USA Today*, plus most of the recruiting tracking services, called the top class in the nation. The plum was Chris Simms, son of Giants great Phil Simms, from Franklin Lakes, New Jersey. Simms had announced a commitment to Tennessee, but Brown convinced him to sign with Texas. Viewed from the perspective of the Texas-OU game and all that encompasses, the Brown-Simms bonding would become a partnership of grief and sorrow. In the off-season of Brown's recruiting haul, a third character essential in the modern-day Texas-OU drama had walked onto the stage.

The previous decade of football had been a cruel one in Norman. After Barry Switzer left the program, that so-called shadow-of-greatness syndrome would take hold at OU. Switzer's act would not soon be followed, not in the fashion that Oklahoma fans craved. Gary Gibbs, promoted to take over for Switzer, lost to Texas in his first try, and his second, and his third. And these were not outstanding Texas teams. Gary was a goner. OU made the curious choice of Howard Schnellenberger, a veteran coach who looked like a 350-pound Captain Kangaroo. He lasted a year. Then came John Blake, who lost twenty-two out of thirty-four games. For Oklahomans, this test of faith had gone on long enough.

Salvation was at hand with the hiring of Bob Stoops. A son of the Rust Belt, schooled in the Corn Belt, and seasoned in the boiling hot grease of southern-fried football, Stoops was ready to retool the Sooners' long-dormant battlewagon. His reputation among the coaching underground ranked Stoops as the most promising candidate for future notoriety in the profession. After one season of charting the defense for Steve Spurrier's Florida Gators, Stoops was offered the head coach's post at Pitt. He declined. "I've only been at Florida a year," he said at the time. "And now I'm supposed to ride Coach Spurrier's coattails and bail out?" Eager and confident, Stoops finally left Steve Spurrier's acclaimed program to accept the Oklahoma project, that of Sooner Renewal. The job was real, and it was big. Stoops set his jaw and said, "There should be great expectations here. It is the program with championships that should expect championships. We know we will operate with no excuses. There are no excuses. Either you succeed or you don't." Barry Switzer was one who thought that Stoops would finally be the person who could not only withstand the heat of the Sooner kitchen but actually thrive in it. "You can see this guy has what it takes," said Switzer. "He's got the personality, the smarts, the toughness . . . clearly a young man who didn't need to be shown things more than once."

At OU, Stoops thought of himself at once as a person who had gone to heaven without yet dying. The atmosphere that everyone breathed around the Norman area contained 90 percent football, 9 percent oxygen and 1 percent noxious gases that blew across the Red River from Texas. The campus provided a golf course that enabled Stoops to play a quick nine holes during his lunch break and a bar called Louie's that served his favorite cocktail, Jim Beam and Red Bull. "You have everything that a coach can look for here," he said. "This is a place where it is easy to stay a long time."

Also, the job put him in immediate proximity with some of the best college football players in the country whose abilities had been squandered by the unfocused coaching administrations that preceded Stoops. Fact was, while Texas was savoring some success against Oklahoma throughout the 1990s, the UT coaches privately felt that "the team over on the other side of the tunnel had more talent."

Stoops lost his first encounter with Mack Brown in Dallas. By 1998, the Texas-OU weekend was an atmosphere in decline, with both programs having been in the doldrums for a decade. The frantic Friday-night downtown revelries were now a part of the past. Finally, somebody had gotten shot and the pregame celebrants had been quarantined into the tidy West End restaurant-and-bar district. OU fans, lusting for a revival of previous glories, watched gleefully as the Sooners carried the fight to Brown's Steers and claimed a first-half 17–0 lead. From there, the game turned into a rout. For Texas. Behind Major Applewhite, the Longhorns awakened, then defeated the Stoops's crimson-clad team, 38–28.

Brown felt that his Longhorns would beat the Sooners again in 2000. UT had played sloppily in an early game, losing at Stanford while Tiger Woods stood on the Cardinal sideline, cheering for his school. Representing a state renowned for its equal-opportunity prison death-house in Huntsville, one would think that the Texas football team could execute better. The coach was sure that his engine was in tune for the match with OU. He felt good about the state of his program in Austin. Simms, alternating at quarterback with Applewhite, owned the strongest passing arm ever to wear the burnt orange. UT's three freshman receivers were a trio of absolute gems. Roy Williams was an uncut forty-carat diamond, and B. J. Johnson and Sloan Thomas had been appraised as pure sapphire. Furthermore, the Longhorns had received an early commitment from a player largely deemed the best high school running back in the United States, Cedric Benson from Midland. Brown was certain that his Texas team was poised to dominate the Big 12 and advance into a ceaseless procession of BSC championship game appearances.

All of those ambitions evaporated in a single afternoon. While Mack Brown was tabulating the strength of his resources before the OU game, Bob Stoops, about to spring the greatest sneak attack in the history of the series, addressed his team before the energy-charged march down the Cotton Bowl tunnel and onto the battlefield. "You can't be in awe of Texas," Stoops told his players. "You are one of the elite teams. You are Oklahoma. We fully expect you to win this game and a lot more."

Stoops's Sooners, with a quarterback from that football hotbed of South Dakota and a running back maybe not tall enough to board all of the rides at Disney World, whipped the Longhorns like a redheaded stepchild; beat 'em like a rented mule. The day was a glorious rebirth of the Sooners as a national power and a living nightmare for the Longhorns. Mike Tyson, in his prime, never leveled an opponent like OU did Texas; UT was defenseless against the flurry of Oklahoma punches. OU defenders like

Andre Woolfolk, Rocky Calmus, and Roy Williams (a Sooners defensive back, not the UT pass catcher) were unblocked through the course of the game, while most of the OU people carrying the football went untackled. Josh Heupel, the OU quarterback, could stand untouched and select his target.

His Texas counterparts, Applewhite and Simms, found it difficult to complete passes to the prize freshman receivers. When a quarterback gets knocked on his ass before he can even set his feet to throw, it messes up a team's offensive timing. Numbers don't lie, and with five minutes still to play in the first half, Brown and his team had to ponder numbers such as these: First downs: OU 16, Texas 1. Total yards: OU 271, Texas 62. Score: OU 42, Texas 0. Brown was on the emergency phone to NASA headquarters: "Austin, we've got a problem."

Chris Simms summed up Texas's day succinctly. "They kept on scoring, and we kept on punting," he said.

Oklahoma won, finally, 63–14. The not-quite-five-foot-seven halfback Quentin Griffin made touchdown runs of one, two, four, three, eight, and one yards. That makes six. Back in the 1960s, when Darrell Royal was doing things right, the entire Oklahoma team managed a total of five touchdowns against Texas in *seven* years. Now, this one little guy scored six in a single game. "I guess you'd have to call this a career day," said Griffin.

If Texas didn't belong on the same field with these Sooners, then who did? The answer was nobody. The Dallas cycle was reinventing itself. Having successfully constructed a team that could prevail in the State Fair showdown, Stoops had him a team that would prevail anywhere. OU upset Florida State in the Orange Bowl, and in his second season, Stoops had a national championship. While Bob Stoops was telling the OU fans that this masterpiece was the prelude overture to his new-millennium grand football opera, Brown was preparing for an autopsy. That might take a while because crash scene investigators were still searching for the black box. The ladies and gentlemen of the mainstream media would be getting tacky now. "How long does the honeymoon last?" demanded a Dallas columnist. "Who is the starting quarterback?"

Brown, hoarse and glassy-eyed, said, "I want to apologize to all the Texas fans, our players, and our assistant coaches, because I obviously did a poor job of coaching this week." Thus would begin a new Longhorn tradition. Get your balls kicked off by the Oklahoma Sooners, win the remainder of the regular season games, and travel on to San Diego and an appointment in the Holiday Bowl. The carryover effect from the 2000 game—remembered in infamy around Austin as the Mauling at the Midway—would linger for four more dreadful State Fair weekends to come. Stoops, radiant, smug, and smiling, would gaze across the field at the psychologically humbled foe. His look said it all: *We own you fuckers.*

If anything of value came from the wreckage of the 2000 game in Dallas, it was this: The week that Texas was enduring the humiliation of the drubbing, UT assistant coach Oscar Giles had established contact with a tall and promising high school quarterback, still a junior, at Madison High in Houston. The kid told the Texas recruiter that if the offer was there, he wanted to become a Longhorn. And as Texas coaches would discover on a variety of future occasions, Vince Young meant exactly what he said.

Tom Garrison owns what is Dallas's most enduringly popular restaurant-bar operation. It's called the Stoneleigh P. The building that houses the bar used to be a drugstore, across from the venerable old Stoneleigh Hotel on Maple Avenue, near down-town. The neon sign that once had read "Stoneleigh Pharmacy" had partially burned out. The -*harmacy* part was gone, thus the name of Garrison's restaurant. Garrison has taped a clipping from the *New York Times,* listing his hamburger as the best in the United States, to his front door. Through the years, the P has attracted a colorful assortment of regulars, ranging from Donald Rumsfeld to Lauren Bacall. More than a successful purveyor of food and booze, Tom Garrison considers himself first and fore-most a graduate of the University of Oklahoma. On the night before the 2005 Texas-OU game, his joint filled with people wearing orange shirts and talking too loudly, Garrison looked at me and said, "Most every bar owner in Dallas right now is hop-ing to God that Oklahoma wins. Because when we lose, all of the OU fans leave town before sundown."

Garrison pointed across the street at the Stoneleigh Hotel. "My father ... who hated Darrell Royal for coming to Texas and called him a traitor ... would come down to Dallas and stay over there. He'd register for two nights, and whenever Oklahoma lost, it was always the same goddamn thing. He would rush back to the hotel and check out, telling the front-desk guy, 'I've got an emergency back at the house.' Hanging around this town after getting beat by Texas was more than his pride could tolerate."

The chances of OU fans celebrating deep into Saturday night didn't look good before the 2005 game. The Sooners, who had graduated a Heisman Trophy–winning quarterback, Jason White, and shipped a vanload of talent to the NFL, hit an early-season slump. They'd lost their opener to TCU—the silence in the sta-dium at Norman resounding as the clock expired with the Frogs on top, 17–10. OU went to Pasadena and got roughed up by UCLA. That was a bad trip for the Sooners fans who traveled to

California. After the game, some Bruins fans yelled at OU loyalists, "We just kicked your ass, and we don't even give a shit about football."

OU fans listened to the same sort of crap from UT people as they marched nervously into the Cotton Bowl. Adrian Peterson, the greatest runner in the world, was sidelined with a bad ankle. Texas, on the other hand, had gone on the road and defeated Ohio State, so the Longhorns looked suspiciously like a team that might win the national championship.

This contest was no contest at all. Vince Young was a player from another galaxy. Texas won, 45–12, and the one hundredth Texas-OU game was cataloged and pressed into the archives.

The enduring spirit of the people who make this weekend so majestically unreal still prevailed. As the Texans and Okies milled about the fairground after the football game, one woman scoffed at the audacity of the State Fair people, trying to charge a buck and a half to view an albino rattlesnake.

"Albino rattlesnake?" the woman said in a beautiful soprano Red River voice. "Shit fire. I was married to one for seventeen years."

11

Ten Great Players

A list of the one thousand best players from the Texas-OU game would be an injustice to an additional thousand who were just as good. The assembly here, for instance, excludes four Heisman Trophy winners. Names appearing on this list were selected virtually at random from a legion of participants whose "above and beyond" performances lie at the heart-and-soul foundation of the October bloodbath.

BOBBY LAYNE, UNIVERSITY OF TEXAS

As a pro with the Lions and Steelers, the tagline on Layne was that he never lost a game. Occasionally time ran out on him. Layne never seemed to encounter any such problems in his off-the-field life. Closing time never came.

That pattern was in place as part of Layne's routine as soon as he'd set foot on the UT campus in 1944, fresh from a stint with the Merchant Marines. Layne had been a high school teammate of Doak Walker's at Highland Park in Dallas. He arrived in Austin amid high expectations. Then Layne missed his first practice.

Dana X. Bible, the coach, was old-school. He said, "Bobby, where in the world were you?"

Layne looked at Bible and said, "Coach, you don't *even want to know.*"

Bible, understanding the nature of the leadership potential of his bloodshot freshman, shrugged and nodded, and from then on, never troubled himself to inquire of Bobby's whereabouts.

Later in life, Bobby Layne would be cited in West Texas for a misdemeanor involving vice and an undercover cop. Layne represented himself in court, claiming that he was illegally entrapped. "Being who I am, it's just not fair," Layne told the judge. "Because if you set the trap, you'll catch old Bobby every time."

The kinds of traps that Bud Wilkinson needed to stop Layne weren't allowed on the football field. Texas beat Oklahoma all four years that Layne played, and Wilkinson didn't begin to build his success story in Dallas until Layne was gone.

JERRY TUBBS, UNIVERSITY OF OKLAHOMA

Joe Kerbel is what they call a coaching legend in Texas. Near the end of his career at West Texas State, Kerbel, confined to a golf cart because of gout, sped after the officials following a game against North Texas, shaking his fist and screaming obscenities. By that point in his life, Kerbel had mellowed. Back in the early days, when Kerbel was coaching at Breckenridge High, even in an occupation in which grown men blow whistles and scream at people all day, everybody said Joe was a crazy man.

When Jerry Tubbs was in high school, playing for Joe Kerbel, he never lost a game. When visiting teams came to Breckenridge, townspeople would pelt their buses with rocks, coming and leaving. Maybe it was easy for Tubbs to go unbeaten in high school. Nobody who played against the Buckaroos ever had the guts to try to win.

In any case, Tubbs was a hardened veteran when he got to

Oklahoma, and he never lost a game there, either, without the benefit of any rock-throwing supporters. Tubbs was surrounded by all-star talent. Bo Bolinger. Ed Gray. Max Boydston. Kurt Burris. None ever played better than Tubbs, particularly in the 1955 Texas game.

Tubbs intercepted three Longhorn passes and was credited with twenty tackles. OU won 20–0. Texas gained sixty-seven yards rushing. The next year, Tubbs led a Sooners defense that shut out Texas again, this time 45–0. Tubbs would have to eventually travel all the way to San Francisco, about as far from Breckenridge as a person can get, before experiencing the sensation of being on the losing side of a game. That finally happened in a preseason game with the Forty-Niners.

BOB KALSU, UNIVERSITY OF OKLAHOMA

Members of the freshman class who came to Oklahoma in the fall of 1964 might remember their years in Norman as, if not the worst of times, then certainly the most unsettled. In three varsity seasons, the group would play for three different head coaches. Gomer Jones was fired after the 1965 season. Jim Mackenzie, leader of a regime change imported from Arkansas, died suddenly after his only season in 1966.

Throughout, Bob Kalsu viewed the situation involving not only Oklahoma football but the world at large with knowing, benign, and optimistic eyes. "Whenever I watch replays of *Night Court,* I think of Bob Kalsu," said a contemporary. "The character of the bailiff, Nostradamus 'Bull' Shannon—that was Bob. Big, easygoing, always grinning. That was Bob." From all accounts, Kalsu never entered a room that he didn't light up.

Kalsu, a product of Del City, Oklahoma, was a key lineman in the 1966 game, when Oklahoma finally broke Texas's eight-game winning streak in Dallas. That game was the only break in a seemingly endless drought against the Longhorns that extended thirteen years. Under Mackenzie's replacement, Chuck Fairbanks, Kalsu's senior group lost a close game to Texas, but that was the only one. Kalsu was named first-team all-American. The day after the Orange Bowl, Kalsu married his girlfriend, Judy. He was drafted in the eighth round by Buffalo, then surprised the team by starting.

A rising star, Kalsu, member of an ROTC unit, abandoned pro football to fulfill his military obligation.

On July 23, 1970, Lieutenant Kalsu was killed by an exploding mortar shell at a place called Firebase Ripcord in Vietnam. Judy was informed of his death three hours after the birth of her second child, Robert Kalsu Jr. Kalsu was the only player in the National Football League to die in action in the Vietnam conflict. The high school stadium in Del City is named in his memory.

BILLY SIMS, UNIVERSITY OF OKLAHOMA

Coach Barry Switzer, a self-proclaimed silver-tongued devil when it came to the art of recruiting salesmanship, listed the job he did on Billy Sims as his all-time personal best.

Sims was a perfect candidate for stardom in the Texas-Okahoma series, being an employee of Big Oil. Actually, Sims was working at a Conoco station on a highway outside of Hooks, Texas, hidden in the deep woods of the eastern part of the state where few humans choose to tread.

The halfback from the sticks received a phone call from Switzer at the gas station on a Saturday afternoon. The OU coach was on the job that afternoon, too. He was calling Sims from a pay phone in the locker room at Boulder. The Sooners were pounding Colorado so decisively that Switzer could not resist the urge to phone his prize candidate for future backfield stardom and tell him all about it. He encouraged Sims to tune in to the second half of the game on the radio and told him what plays the Sooners would run in the final thirty minutes. The only reason Switzer didn't get a firm commitment on the pay phone was that he ran out of quarters.

Sims became the chief cog in a college football dream backfield, occasionally sharing the top billing with David Overstreet, Thomas Lott, and Kenny King. As a junior in 1978, Sims won the Heisman Trophy. That season would be Sims's only win in four tries against the Longhorns. Oklahoma won decisively, 31–10, with Sims scoring an important, albeit disputed touchdown when the ball popped out of his hands as he dived across the goal line.

He gained 131 yards on twenty-five carries that day. As Sims accepted the award as ABC's Player of the Game, he said, "This is great. The only thing I wish is that Darrell Royal was still the Texas coach, so we could have humiliated him along with the Longhorns."

Sims was runner-up to Charles White for the Heisman in 1979 and was the MVP of the Orange Bowl game in his final appearance as an Oklahoma Sooner. He was voted into the College Football Hall of Fame in 1995.

TOMMY NOBIS, UNIVERSITY OF TEXAS

The most notable physical characteristic of the most fearsome player of the entire Darrell Royal reign in Austin was his neck. By the standards of his time, Tommy Nobis was not a huge man. But his neck was. Nobis wore shirts with size nineteen collars.

Another thing that Nobis wore was the constant expression of a man who'd just discovered that his pickup had been stolen, with all his tools in the back, and he knew the polecat who'd taken it. In other words, infuriated and eager to settle the score. Nobis moved from sideline to sideline with the grace of a puma.

When Nobis collided with a ball carrier—according to teammate Tommy Ford—the runner was greeted with the sensation of having performed a high dive into an empty swimming pool. The redheaded attack-bomber from San Antonio was as unstoppable in his desire to improve as he was on the football field.

Royal was not an advocate of weight training when he first came to Texas. Nobis, through assistant coaches, lobbied for the establishment of a first-class weight room in Austin. He got his way.

Texas's big win over the Sooners in 1963—Nobis's sophomore season—was the game in which he established his all-American credentials. In his final two seasons in Austin, Nobis wouldn't play on any more national championships, but when his college career was over after the 1965 season, three years would have passed and Oklahoma still hadn't blocked him.

In three tries against a Nobis-led Longhorn defense, Oklahoma would score two touchdowns and never attain double-digit first downs. In fact, as a senior, Nobis and his teammates blanked the Sooners 19–0, and limited OU to only six first downs.

PETER GARDERE, UNIVERSITY OF TEXAS

Five years had passed since Texas had beaten Oklahoma when the Longhorns took the field against the Sooners in 1989. Texas didn't appear to have a chance, particularly with a freshman quarterback whose last name was best known for the major big-city law firm that his grandfather had cofounded. So Texas had a guy genetically geared to collect billable hours, which does not necessarily correlate to beating OU.

Barry Switzer was gone at last, but when the Sooners ran onto the Cotton Bowl floor, it was evident that the men in the red helmets were on their customary Dallas mission. I was in the stands (not the press box) for the first time in a quarter of a century, and when Gardere trotted out for the Longhorns' first possession, I was among 75,000 spectators who were all think-ing the same thing: *This poor guy is fixin' to get himself killed.*

Instead, Gardere, seemingly unaware of the howling mael-strom that engulfed him from all sides, casually directed a long touchdown drive. Texas led at the half. Like most of the spec-tators, I rushed outside to the nearest State Fair beer stand, where an OU fan wearing a blank expression said, "This is a nightmare," to nobody in particular. In the second half, nature would take it course, and the Sooners forged a 24–21 lead. The sounds coming from the OU side were cheers of relief, not exultation.

Little Peter wasn't finished, though. With a little more than a minute to play, Gardere fired a twenty-seven-yard pass that Johnny Walker, leaping in the end zone, snatched from the hand of an OU defender. Texas won, 28–24. While the UT band boomed "Eyes of Texas" and the orange-shirted fans flooded the field, I actually saw an old Longhorn fan standing and wiping tears from his cheeks with a corny-dog wrapper.

Gardere never stopped. Not against the Sooners, anyway. In four starts, Gardere won four games. James Street never accom-plished that. Or Vince Young. Only Bobby Layne. As Gardere stood on the sidelines in 1992, with Texas ahead and the game in the bag, OU fans began a chant directed at the smiling QB. "Graduate!" they demanded. "Graduate!"

BRIAN BOSWORTH, UNIVERSITY OF OKLAHOMA

Kathy Bosworth, the linebacker's mother, watched from the stands at Mile High Stadium as her son Brian, youngest of three and playing for the Seattle team, was led off the field protected by cops. Bosworth had trashed the Broncos in newspaper quotes earlier in the week, enraging Denver fans. "If Brian had been the oldest, he'd have been the only," sighed Kathy. During the week before the Denver game, Bosworth had told a wire service reporter about "wanting to get my claws in John Elway's boyish face."

"I've learned why he says those things," said Bosworth's mom, "but I still cringe and think, 'Oh Lord . . . they're going to get him.'"

The rap on Brian Bosworth came down to this. Brash. Arrogant. Bigmouthed. A total bust as a professional football player, and even at that, his NFL reviews were better than the ones Bosworth received as a screen actor.

His college coach, Barry Switzer, did not damn Bosworth with faint praise after he left Norman. Switzer offered no praise at all. "The Boz was an asshole who walked around Norman like he owned the place, both stiffing and intimidating people."

But there was another side to the Boz, the one who had taken one look at Owen Field in Norman and "gotten goose bumps the size of golf balls . . . and when I saw the weight room, I was hooked."

OU may have had better football players than Brian Bosworth, certainly players who left a more positive legacy. Oklahoma, though, will never put a player into the State Fair wars who hated Texas as much as Bosworth. The Boz had grown up in Irving, Texas, home of the Dallas Cowboys, and everything about the stadium—with the hole in the roof, and the team in silver and blue—made him "want to puke."

Bosworth, wearing number forty-four, had a special grudge against the Longhorns. He personally dismantled the Texas attack in the 1985 game, and again the following season. The Boz became the first player to win the Butkus Award twice, and he finished his tenure at OU with 395 tackles. On top of that, Bosworth became an academic all-American. Switzer pointed out that the only thing Bosworth loved was his hair, but the Boz's lack of love for Texas and everything it represented was something that OU fans should cherish forever.

RICKY WILLIAMS, UNIVERSITY OF TEXAS

Mack Brown, acknowledged as the master recruiter, has pulled more than his share of marquee names to Austin. Brown still insists that his best effort didn't involve a high school blue-chip stud. The object of Brown's ardent persuasive powers was a player already on the Austin campus—Ricky Williams, the man with Mickey Mouse tattooed on his right bicep. The man with the trademark dreadlocks. The Rambling Rasta.

Williams was due a big check from the pros after his junior season at Texas, having convinced scouts of his readiness to play and dominate in the Sunday league. Brown convinced Ricky Williams to stick around for his senior season—both for the good of the player and the good of the coach, who was staring into the face of a shambles of an inaugural season without Williams.

"There're certain things that money can't buy, like camaraderie and the team being together, and loyalty," said Williams, echoing Brown's pitch, after he'd decided to stick with the college game one more year.

Williams had already won the Doak Walker Award as the country's best runner. Then playing against Oklahoma in the so-called House That Doak Built, Williams enjoyed an afternoon against the Sooners that cemented his bid for the Heisman Trophy. Doak Walker, a person whom Williams had met and admired, had been paralyzed before the start of the 1998 season in a skiing accident, and later died.

Williams wore Walker's old number—thirty-seven—in his senior year. After he had trampled the Sooners with more than 130 yards and two TDs (a third, a seventy-eight-yard run, was nullified by a penalty), Williams gave his sweaty jersey to members of Walker's family who attended the game.

JASON WHITE, UNIVERSITY OF OKLAHOMA

How—playing for a true coaching genius like Bob Stoops and surrounded by a full entourage of NFL talent—could a quarterback like White *not* win the Heisman Trophy?

Certain critics, otherwise known as the ink-stained wretches and talking dogs who earn a living by casting judgments from their elevated perches in the press box, downgraded White's abilities. Why go overboard about a guy who mans the controls of a machine that seemed to fly perfectly well on automatic pilot?

The 2003 Sooners juggernaut, at the end of the regular season, had certain media backers claiming this was the best college team ever assembled. Then, against Kansas State in the Big 12 championship game, White sustained a shoulder injury. It was bad. White stayed on the field, but guess what? With White's timing off and his play-making abilities impaired, Oklahoma was not the same team. The Sooners lost to K-State and then against LSU in the BSC championship game.

White, as it turned out, was a helluva college player who saved his best efforts for Dallas and the Texas Longhorns. White engineered a laugher in the 2003 game, a 65–13 blowout. In his last game against the Horns, White was pitted against a player named Vince Young, who was deemed the more talented quarterback by far. In the end, Young made mistakes. White didn't, and Oklahoma beat Texas, 12–0, for the fifth consecutive season.

JAMES STREET, UNIVERSITY OF TEXAS

Thirty-three high school football stand-outs from Texas, including quarterback James Street, traveled to Hershey in 1966 to play against a Pennsylvania team in an all-star game.

The week that practices began, the two coaches met and made a gentleman's agreement. No blitzing. In the game, Texas blitzed all night long. The Texans won by a lopsided score, embarrassed the Pennsylvanians, and were never invited back. Interestingly, the coach of the Texas team was Bobby Layne, the old UT quarterback who won over Oklahoma in four tries out of four.

Layne's ethic: When it comes to winning a football game, a man's gotta do what a man's gotta do.

James Street might not have learned that lesson from Layne, but he learned it somewhere. Darrell Royal and Emory Bellard may have invented the Wishbone T, but it was James Street who taught them how to play with it and have fun. Street saved his best performances for the Carnegie Hall of Lone Star football, the Cotton Bowl. Both on New Year's Day and during the State Fair, Street came through with flair. Beating Oklahoma in that annual October thrombosis is difficult enough, but coming from behind to beat the Sooners—while not unheard of—is rare. Street did it twice.

If Notre Dame's grandeur was founded on the Four Horsemen, then Texas owes every bit as much to the original Wishbone T backfield: Three Horsemen and a Hustler.

12

Ten Great Games

For the fans of the winning team any one of the one hundred installments of the Texas-Oklahoma football series might rank as a classic. It is important to note that I am not claiming this as a "Ten Greatest" list. In a series like Texas-OU, there is no such thing. The selections included here are games the author attended in person, and the expressions of the fans' faces cheering for the victorious side always confirmed that this was an afternoon they would never forget.

1950—OKLAHOMA 14, TEXAS 13

My grade school years were enhanced considerably because of college football.

My father had watched the 1949 Notre Dame–SMU game on a television set at the Officers Club at Carswell Air Force Base in Fort Worth, where the wreckage of the mysterious Roswell flying saucer was stored in a hangar. Television was practically nonexistent, but Mr. Fort Worth himself, Amon Carter, was far ahead of the curve when it came to innovation. A skeptical man not prone to offer idle praise, my father came home with rave notices, both about the game and the quality of the telecast on

Amon Carter's Channel 5. "You could see the expressions on the players' faces," he said, and the next week, he went and bought a twelve-inch Philco console. We were among the first people in town to own a set. Given my father's frugal propensities, if it hadn't been for the football game, we would have been the last.

The Texas-Oklahoma game wasn't televised in 1950. A film of the game was shown the next day, every play to the background music of the Colonial Bogey March. No graphics. No replays. No sideline commentator. It was a great way to watch a football game. Grainy black-and-white film on a TV signal that came and went; the ferocity of the day-old fight still reached out from the screen. Clearly, the action was more authentic than the live-action studio wrestling shows.

Those wrestling programs at least carried a script that was more legit than the propaganda that Bud Wilkinson had put out the week before the game. Bud's team was number one in the wire-service polls, Texas one slot beneath. "On paper, the only department in which we are as good as they is courage," Wilkinson wrote in his weekly newsletter, inciting the fear factor statewide in Oklahoma.

"We're lucky if Texas doesn't run us down the field. We will be playing one of the finest teams in the nation, and the only possible way we can beat them is to play over our heads—again." A great coach, Wilkinson liked to lay it on thick. The Longhorns gave him reason to. Bud McFadin, a tackle, was a legitimate all-American. And Texas had beaten Purdue, which had turned around and beaten Notre Dame—OU's rival at the top of the national polls.

The contest was a bloody stalemate throughout. Bobby Dillon, the one-eyed all-American, intercepted a pass and returned it forty-five yards for a touchdown, to break a 7–7 tie. Billy Porter missed the conversion. Oklahoma made the winning touchdown when Billy Vessels, Heisman Trophy winner two years later, ran eleven yards. Jim Weatherall, the first Texan from White Deer (which is as remote as it sounds), kicked the winning extra point.

Throughout the following week, everybody in Austin claimed the Longhorns had gotten screwed by the zebras on a couple of key plays. Blair Cherry, the coach, went public and encouraged Texas supporters to get over it and move on. Maybe Cherry was able to, even though it cost him his job, but when I went to school in Austin a decade later, people were still bitching about how Lew Levine got shafted out of his second-quarter touchdown.

That's one of the dubious features of the Texas-OU thing. One bad afternoon in the Cotton Bowl can leave you scarred for life.

1952—OKLAHOMA 49, TEXAS 20

The National Football League came to Dallas and installed a team called the Texans that vanished without a trace. In 1952, there were more registered members of the Communist Party, probably, than fans of the NFL. Browns versus Eagles? Who gave a damn? The NFL was a Sunday activity that existed only for the American gaming industry. Texans would rather watch roller derby than pro football because the fights seemed more authentic.

The college game was all that mattered on the sports pages. Then, in Austin, Notre Dame made a rare and heralded appearance, and the people at Memorial Stadium weren't sure if they were watching a football game or a Tarzan movie. All of the pregame speculation had been that the Irish couldn't withstand the Texas heat. And it was unseasonably warm that day; the players on the field felt like they were in an adobe oven. So over on the sunny side of the UT bull ring, Notre Dame coach Frank Leahy—Bud Wilkinson's only genuine rival as the best football coach in America—outfitted his team with pith helmets. What a knee-slapper. Notre Dame won, 14–3, and Frank Leahy said, "I think the heat got to Texas."

With Texas coach Blair Cherry ousted, bitter and complaining of respiratory problems (that god-awful mountain cedar had gotten to him), his replacement Ed Price took one of the best-decorated teams in UT history to play Oklahoma. Tackle Harley Sewell and end Tom Stolhanske were consensus all-Americans. For the first and last time in the history of the Southwest Conference, all four all-conference backs came from the same team: Gib Dawson, T. Jones, Richard Ochoa, and Billy Quinn. Two other linemen, Bill Georges and Phil Branch, were all-conference as well.

They ran the table in the SWC and beat Tennessee in the Cotton Bowl. And they couldn't stay on the same field with Oklahoma. In a court of law, the Longhorns might have entered a no-contest plea, paid a fine, and gone on. But this was football, and so they had to go face Billy Vessels, Eddie Crowder, Buck McPhail, Tom Catlin, and some other Oklahoma players who didn't make all-American but were just as good, and get their asses stomped. Oklahoma, behind freshman quarterback Buddy Leake, scored almost at will.

The Sooners' surge left an imprint that defined a sports decade throughout two states—that October belonged to the New York Yankees and the Oklahoma Sooners.

1959—TEXAS 19, OKLAHOMA 12

In the springtime of my junior year in high school, a narrow spinning funnel—dark and vengeful—came from the sky and demolished a soon-to-be-occupied orphanage on a hilltop across the street from the school. Blew the building into—and I'm not exaggerating here—a million little pieces. The funnel went back up, barely missing the high school. I watched that happen from a vantage point that, from my perspective, was too damn close to the center of the action.

I figured that episode would do nicely as a personal snapshot that would last a lifetime. Then the following October came around, and I realized that my run-in with a Texas twister was nothing more than a cheap thrill. For the first time, I attended a Texas-OU game, sitting on the upper deck in the east side of the Cotton Bowl in the Oklahoma section. The atmosphere at those TCU games I'd been attending, good as the Horned Frogs had been, was choir practice in comparison to the delirium on display in Dallas. This spectacle doesn't merely assault the senses; it sodomizes 'em and then beats 'em to death.

On the field and in the stands, the gamut of emotions taught at the best acting school in the world would have been expended by the middle of the first quarter. Every big play, and those were mostly provided by the defense, was greeted in the stands with the resounding, concussive effect of a cherry bomb exploding in a garbage can.

The Sooners fans in my section were jumping, literally, with joy as OU took the field and right away began kicking the boys in orange where it hurt the most. Bob Cornell threw a touchdown pass to Jackie Holt, and Dick Carpenter tight-roped the sideline on a thirty-eight-yard TD trip, and the Sooners went ahead, 12–0.

OU people had come away from the last year's game, Darrell Royal's 15–14 win, feeling ambushed and shortchanged. Texas was supposed to *lose these goddamn games*, I heard the guy sitting behind me say. The mood of the Oklahoma fans, as the Sooners took the lead early, might best have been described as retaliatory. And they rejoiced in the fact that Prentice Gautt—the Sooners' first African-American player—was leading the

Oklahoma stampede. "God, don't you know those Texas assholes just hate this," the guy behind me said. "Listen to 'em. I bet that instead of 'block that kick,' it's 'kick that black.'"

Royal's team made a comeback. They scored after a long drive. An ex-quarterback, Rene Ramirez, dubbed by the brilliant media as the galloping gaucho, threw a left-handed halfback pass to Larry Cooper for a score. Texas took the lead right at the end of the half when Mike Dowdle scored from the one. The people in my section were convinced that the referee had stopped the clock improperly before the TD. I'd heard of a game in the late 1940s when the Sooners pelted the game officials with whiskey bottles. Nobody heaved any bottles—my section was too far from the field—but the mood was right.

Jack Collins, a hometown hero from Highland Park, made a sixty-five-yard touchdown in the third quarter that enlivened the Texas side. Late in the game, when it was evident that the Sooners were doomed after a diving interception at the UT eight by Mike Cotten, the chant began. "Poor Okie."

The chant grew more prolonged, and loud. "P-o-o-o-r Ohhh-Keeee!"

"For Chrissakes," said the guy. "Give us a break."

That game was the fifty-third of the Texas-OU series. I would wager that somebody in the Cotton Bowl had seen every game to that point, and I know there are people who have attended every game since. So in the stands that day were probably two people who, combined, now have attended all one hundred.

1983—TEXAS 28, OKLAHOMA 16

The decade of the 1970s was remembered as the time of the immortal running back in the Texas-Oklahoma series. Earl Campbell and Billy Sims rated at the top of the list of headline magnets who won Heisman trophies. The next ten years, though, would have to be characterized as the dark days of promise unfilled.

Marcus Dupree was perhaps the greatest coup in Barry Switzer's tenure in Norman. Dupree came from Philadelphia, Mississippi, and Switzer, seeing Dupree's 230-pound frame and amazing speed, deemed him Hercules. As a freshman, Dupree contributed mightily to the Sooners' cause, and his sixty-three touchdowns against Texas had keyed OU's 28–22 win in the 1982 game.

The off-season was not productive, however. Dupree caused Switzer unending angst by sitting out spring practice with a variety of physical complaints. During the summer, according to the coach, Dupree had gone home to Mississippi and devoted three months to a training routine that consisted of eating fried chicken.

Marcus, entering his sophomore season, was not quite the player who had arrived in Norman a year earlier. Now Texas came into the game with a Dupree facsimile, Edwin Simmons, a long-striding marvel from East Texas who'd watched the '82 game on television from his job at a beauty parlor. Texas had its focus on a run for the national championship, having won convincingly on the road at Auburn in its season opener. In the process, the Longhorns had buried Bo Jackson, who afterward said, "I feel like I've been run over by a herd of cows."

Oklahoma, naturally, was ready for the Longhorns' best shot. The Sooners, like they always seemed to, took charge after the opening kickoff. OU scored first, when quarterback Danny Bradley scrambled out of a trap in his backfield, then threw on the run to Steve Sewell for an eight-yard touchdown. Simmons scored for Texas and tied the game at the half. A key play happened in the third quarter. Bradley threw a slant-pattern pass to

Buster Rhymes, who was open and geared to go the distance. Instead, the ball bounced off Rhymes's hands, and UT's Mossy Cade snatched the interception that led to UT's taking the lead.

Then Edwin Simmons broke three tackles and sprinted sixty-seven yards for the touchdown that sealed the win. Dupree, on the other hand, was limited to fifty yards on fourteen carries and left the game late with a concussion. "Marcus got the shit knocked out of him on every play," Switzer said. With rumors swirling that Dupree wanted to transfer, Switzer kicked him off the team prior to the Oklahoma State game. The Dupree Era at OU ended before it had really gotten started.

After UT's big win, Switzer said, "Simmons is going to be a great player, and I don't see anybody in the Southwest Conference beating Texas." He was right on the latter observation. But Simmons's place in the sun would endure exactly one more week. In Texas's next game against Arkansas, Simmons sustained a knee injury and would never be the same player. His most memorable legacy in Austin came when Simmons was arrested after taking a nocturnal outdoor stroll with no clothes on.

Texas, as Switzer had projected, won the remainder of its regular season games. All of that was tarnished when a fumbled punt against Georgia in the Cotton Bowl game cost UT the national championship. Afterward, jubilant Bulldog fans kept chanting the final score: "Ten to nine . . . kiss my behind!"

1984—OKLAHOMA 15, TEXAS 15

The world learned one thing that year. If you're going to bring big-time sports to Fair Park, stick to football. Some North Dallas auto enthusiasts of the fat-cat persuasion decided the time was right to introduce earthy South Dallas to the glitz and glamour of Formula 1 Grand Prix racing. And vice versa. That cross-cultural experiment was a farce. The asphalt road-course came up in big chunks, unable to withstand the punishment that comes with July sunshine in Texas. Those European drivers whined even more loudly than their Lotus engines. Across Exhibition Avenue, the people at McDonald's refused to serve any *pommes frites* to the Grand Prix visitors, just out of pure spite. Later, the homeowners in the area threatened to sue the Grand Prix organizers, contending that the racket the cars made had screwed their foundations.

That excursion in nuttiness offered a fitting prelude to the Texas-OU contest. One of the most anticipated match-ups—both teams unbeaten and ranked in the top five (UT being number one)—descended into the oddest contest of the one hundred that have been played as of 2006.

The day of the game brought a deluge of biblical scope. The customarily bright and brilliant skies that characterize the October classic had been overtaken on that day by black and ominous clouds overhead. An omen of a $12-a-barrel calamity lying just ahead. Water was ankle-deep on both benches at game time. Both coaches knew that their best-laid plans had been washed out, too. "Our game is based on finesse and speed, and the weather took that away from us, so we were forced to play error-free ball," said Texas coach Fred Akers.

Texas jumped ahead to a 10–0 lead at the halftime. Todd Dodge threw a twenty-five-yard touchdown to the greatest name in the annals of Longhorn athletics—Bill Boy Bryant. He left a wake as he fell into the end zone. That would be the last anyone would hear of Bill Boy, though. Oklahoma took the field for the second half, well prepared for an aquatic struggle.

They got their break when Keith Stanberry recovered a Texas fumble and Steve Sewell ran a touchdown.

The downpour was getting to the Longhorns. Terry

Steelhammer snapped the ball over the head of punter John Teltschik for a safety. OU scored again and was outplaying Texas in every facet.

With the rain pouring ever harder, Texas startled the Sooners with a fifty-nine-yard run by a freshman, Kevin Nelson, who was stopped at the one. Four plays later, Texas still hadn't scored. Barry Switzer had his team give up an intentional safety, in exchange for field position, cutting the score to OU 15–UT 12. Behind Dodge, Texas got all the way back to the Sooners' fifteen-yard line, with time almost gone. A third-down pass into the end zone was intercepted. Stanberry's play was overruled by a zebra who missed the call. The replays were clear.

Rather than incur further risk, Akers sent Jeff Ward in to kick the field goal that caused the deadlock. A Mexican standoff without any Mexicans. What a drag. In the tunnel afterward, the OU players offered good-natured taunts to the Longhorns for settling on the tie, taunts like "You fuckin' buncha chickenshits!"

Texas, in fact, seemed pleased with the outcome. They'd gotten a tie. Most of the time, a tie is like kissing your sister. In this case, it was more a matter of kissing their reasonably hot stepsister.

1988—OKLAHOMA 28, TEXAS 13

"BEVO HAS AIDS." That declaration was written across the rear window of a new Mercedes with Oklahoma plates seen driving near downtown Dallas on the eve of the game. Recent trips south of the Red River had been growing more gratifying by the year for Sooners fans. Their medical diagnosis of the Longhorns' mascot was clearly off-base. But the football program at Texas was looking sick. Hookworm, maybe.

The Fred Akers era in Austin ended with the Longhorns on the skids. Switzer had buried Akers in his last trip to Dallas, 47–12, and Akers's successor, David McWilliams, had been walloped in his Dallas coaching debut, 44–9. The '88 model Longhorns appeared unsightly when it first appeared in the showroom. A trip to Provo had been a disaster. Texas lost its opener, 47–6, and the season was already seemingly shot. Texas had needed an official to screw North Texas, but good, in a game that the Longhorns won but didn't deserve to, 27–24. Against *North Texas*! And then Texas had squeaked past Rice, 20–13.

Before the Texas game, OU linebacker Karl Kasper, from Houston, said some things to the newspapers that players in this contest aren't supposed to say. But what's wrong with citing the obvious?

"Texas is horrible," Kasper said. "I don't know if Texas could beat Kansas or Kansas State. Don't remind me that I am from Texas. I saw them play BYU, and they just lay down and died."

Oklahoma discovered that Texas, at last, did not come to Dallas to roll over. The Sooners scored a patented Wishbone lightning bolt in the second quarter when Anthony Stafford located a gap in the UT defense, then outran them on an eighty-six-yard touchdown. Somehow, though, the rout was anything but on. Texas was fighting back, or attempting to, behind quarterback Shannon Kelley (who was married to Mary Lou Retton).

Near the end of the first half, Texas began a march, and Karl Kasper felt some unexpected heat. "Of course, when you say something like I said, then you have to go and do something," he conceded.

The unheralded Longhorns evidently had taken some umbrage to his remarks. "They were saying things to us," Kasper said.

Finally Kasper shut them up. He intercepted a Kelley pass and ran it back for a twenty-six-yard TD. "I could hear a couple of coaches yelling at me to lay down, that I was carrying the ball like a loaf of bread," Kasper said. "But I was trying to run north, or whatever direction that was."

Texas still refused to play dead and nearly pulled the play of the game when Kelley threw a pass to Kerry Cash that went eighty yards. Kevin Thompson, who ran a 4.4 forty-yard dash, pulled Cash down at the OU seven. The Sooners held, and UT was forced to kick a field goal.

In the end, OU, sans rout, seemed relieved to have even won. "The difference in the game was that we caught their guy [Cash] and they didn't catch ours [Stafford]," said Barry Switzer. "God, it's always great to win down here."

Switzer didn't realize at the time that this was the final time he'd drink from the UT well. This was his last season—so the Longhorns could chalk up the '88 game as a moral victory.

1990—TEXAS 14, OKLAHOMA 13

After Barry Switzer resigned as Oklahoma's football coach following the 1988 season, Sooners athletic director Donnie Duncan faced the excruciating task of replacing the man who had taken the program and its fans on a sixteen-year thrill ride that featured a hell of a lot more peaks than valleys. Switzer had been the producer-director-screenwriter of *Sooner Magic,* an adventure tale loaded with great escapes and chase scenes in which the resourceful Oklahomans sent the evil Longhorns and Cornhuskers spinning over the side of a cliff. His only theatrical oversight was not handing out pregame eyeglasses so people could watch OU football in 3-D.

The end of the Switzer epic in Norman came with an image quagmire. Was this a college football team for a cartel headquartered somewhere in the Andes? Duncan needed somebody who could bring the assembly-line championships, and he needed someone other than James Bond to accomplish that. Gary Gibbs,

Duncan decided, was the custom-tailored answer. Duncan regarded Gibbs as a decisive leader, a highbrow when it came to gridiron strategy, and a person not inclined to serve as the life of the party at locales like the Remington Park racetrack and Vegas blackjack tables.

After a lukewarm start in his first season, Gibbs finally appeared to find his head-coaching sea legs. Oklahoma was 5-0 coming into the Dallas State Fair cauldron. Cale Gundy from Midwest City, Oklahoma, showed evidence of being a star in the making, and fullback Kenyon Rasheed gave the offense additional clout.

Gibbs's Texas opponent, as had been the custom in the recent renewals of the rivalry, was a team still groping for an offensive identity. David McWilliams, the coach, was a Darrell Royal protégé. Translated, that meant nonflamboyant. McWilliams had been a captain of Royal's first national championship team in 1963. He'd been a math major, with close to an A average. When he graduated, McWilliams sought Royal's counsel on the topic of his career. He'd received a job offer from some company that called itself International Business Machines. Royal told McWilliams that he'd be better off accepting the chance to coach at Abilene High. That's where the job security was.

Now, a generation later, McWilliams found himself in the ulcer pit—the sideline of the Texas-Oklahoma game—the place where job security comes home to die. Texas fans were paying $100 to play in their annual Get Teed Off at OU tournament, causing one entry to wonder, "How come we didn't have a Get Teed Off at Penn State tournament to open the season?"

McWilliams's Longhorns played as expected against the Sooners. Swarming defense. Stalling offense. Texas had managed one decent scoring drive, that in the second quarter. With time running out, the Longhorns were surprised to find themselves trailing only 13–7. Behind quarterback Peter Gardere, Texas mounted a tedious ninety-one-yard drive against a Sooners defense that was beginning to tire.

On fourth-and-seven, UT offensive coordinator Lynn Amedee sent in a play, something called "flex left 60 D." Wide receiver Keith Cash faked outside and cut for the goalpost, and Gardere put the ball in his hands. Oklahoma had time to respond, driving to the Longhorns' thirty before R. D. Lasher came on the field to try the game-winning field goal. UT play-by-play radio announcer Brad Sham called it. "The kick is on the way! It's going . . . going . . . it's *no good!*"

Texas capitalized on the hair-raising climax and won the Southwest Conference championship. Gary Gibbs's program stalled in its tracks after the painful loss. OU would eventually dismiss Gibbs and go through two more head coaches before finding the answer in Bob Stoops.

1994—TEXAS 17, OKLAHOMA 10

John Mackovic could easily have found a good career outside of coaching. Mackovic seemed like a man who was born to model Hathaway shirts. Button-down collars and pinstripes. So it is doubtful that the Texas coach, fretful over switching quarterbacks on the day of the Oklahoma game, realized that he was about to unveil the second coming of the King of Soul.

Shea Morenz had been Mackovic's quarterback ideal, the template of a classic drop-back passer. Morenz was the grandson of Howie Morenz, a hockey legend at Montreal. He'd hurt his knee, though, the week before the OU game, playing against Colorado. Morenz was tough; he'd hidden from the team doctor on the UT bench after he'd injured his leg, fearful he might not be allowed to reenter the game.

His availability against the Sooners was a game-day decision. After the pregame warm-ups and the teams had reentered their dressing rooms, while the din of the bands and howls of the crowd vibrated just outside the door, Mackovic approached James Brown—heretofore a back-up quarterback—and told him in effect that it was showtime.

James Brown would take his first varsity snap ever in the Oklahoma game. Was he all of a sudden nervous? "No," Brown would say later, "I was scared." Then Eric Jackson, a UT wide receiver, told Brown what to expect. "When you take the field, you can feel electricity going through your body. The game's got you in another world. You feel like you're Superman. No one can stop you."

Oklahoma, ranked fifteen nationally, put an early kibosh on any Superman pretensions that Brown might have fostered. The Sooners scored first when Jerald Moore ran twenty-three yards for a TD.

If there was to be any soul to this Texas offense, the man in charge needed to find some rhythm. Gradually, that began to happen. Brown, who eventually connected in seventeen of twenty-two passes, ran eight yards on a third down for a touchdown that put Texas ahead, and he directed another drive that ended on a two-yard TD flip to the tight end, Pat Fitzgerald.

Texas led 17–10 when the Sooners ignited a last-ditch drive. Finally, for the first time in the history of the series, the game hinged on a final play staged from the one-yard line. That's where OU was stationed. While the foundation of the Cotton Bowl began to quake, Oklahoma quarterback Garrick McGee took the snap, headed to his right, then gave the ball to his best halfback, James Allen, on cross-buck. Allen wanted to run outside but saw UT linebacker Robert Reed poised to seal off the corner of the inside. So he cut inside.

Awaiting Allen was a middle guard, Stoney Clark. The term

brick shithouse is a Texas metaphor for a variety of things. Stoney Clark, at just over six feet and just under 340, was built like one. Clark dug his cleats into the turf and awaited Allen's arrival. When the halfback met the lineman head-on, the effect was that of a bug hitting the windshield on the interstate. While the Longhorn defenders ran gleefully off the field, Allen remained on his knees, hands on his helmet. He'd been in a wreck, and Clark had made the defensive play of the decade for the Texas Longhorns.

OU's offensive coordinator was upset after the game. Watson Brown, whose brother Mack would be coaching the Longhorns in four years, said, "I feel sick when I look at a loss like this. And when I look at the stat sheet [where the Sooners had been dominant], it makes me want to throw up."

1999—TEXAS 38, OKLAHOMA 28

The thing about Major Applewhite was not that he looked like the kid next door. He looked like what the parents of the kid next door wished their kid looked like. Wholesome. Trustworthy. Plus, Major had the heart of a tiger and bowling-lane balls. Summoned from the bench after the starter had gone down, Applewhite settled in and made the single best damn play of any UT quarterback in the whole OU series. After Texas had recovered an OU fumble at the lip of its goal line early in the third quarter of the '98 game, the kid they were calling Opie dropped back in his end zone and lofted a perfect rainbow to Wane McGarity, running behind the secondary.

Texas football teams have grown inured to gaining yardage in hiccups in the OU game; such is the year-in-year-out relentlessness of the OU defense when it comes to the Cotton Bowl. Ninety-seven yards on one play was something difficult to fathom. Applewhite led Texas to a massive upset over Nebraska, in Lincoln.

Applewhite's fame would eventually reach national proportions, to the extent that Outsports, a website encompassing "the greater passions of gay and lesbian sports," named an award after him: the Major Applewhite Cutest Quarterback Award, which goes to the college QB "who, like the Major, best shows head, talent and energy in the face of adversity, and cute good looks." Nominees for the 2002 Applewhite Award included Jason Campbell, Ken Dorsey, Kyle Boller (from a family of firefighters), Carson Palmer, and UT's own Chris Simms.

But the fickle fans in Austin were on his case after an early loss to Kansas State. Now it was "Apple Turnover" and "Major Screw-up."

The Sooners saw right away that the Major would require something more than cute looks to win in Dallas. Bob Stoops announced his entry into the Dallas game in what would become customary style. Before either team had broken a sweat, OU, with Josh Heupel throwing long touchdown shots to Antone Savage and Jarrall Jackson, jumped ahead 17–0.

"We stunk at the start," said Brown.

Behind the Major, Texas rallied. Applewhite threw a touchdown to Ryan Nunez and completed a two-point conversion to tie the game at the half.

Two second-half touchdowns, a twenty-one-yard run by Hodges Mitchell and a forty-eight-yard pass to Kwame Cavil, blew the lid off the game. UT fans didn't realize it, but Applewhite had directed a performance that they wouldn't see in Dallas for five long arid years. On the losing side, Bob Stoops was taking notes. He wasn't coming back to this place to lose anymore.

2001—OKLAHOMA 14, TEXAS 3

Mack Brown, one year after the infamous Mauling at the Midway, must have felt like Ted Kennedy at a Chappaquiddick picnic as the Longhorns returned to the Cotton Bowl. Brown had taken on the cheerful demeanor of a man ready to move past the 63–14 Pearl Harbor of a football game that had propelled Oklahoma to its national championship.

Texas, now with Chris Simms at quarterback and Major Applewhite situated on the bench, was actually favored to beat Oklahoma, even though the Sooners seemed every bit as potent as the team that had demolished the Longhorns and everyone else that had gotten in their way. The quarterback spot was the difference. Josh Heupel was gone, and the new guy, Nate Hybl, was considered a downgrade.

Bob Stoops's defensive ensemble was more than ready to take up any slack. Andre Woolfolk. Antonio Perkins. Rocky Calmus. Roy Williams. Teddy Lehman. This wasn't a Big 12 defense. This was a wolf pack, and it would be at its predatory best against a player like Chris Simms. The New Jersey kid had a golden arm, all right, but he was no gazelle.

Simms got very little going against the Sooners defense. Meanwhile, Hybl was injured. It is interesting to note that Stoops had elevated his program to the point that in this hour of crisis, he was able to replace his starter with an eventual Heisman Trophy winner. Jason White led the Sooners to a touchdown near the end of the half.

OU, holding a 7–3 lead, appeared in trouble in the third quarter when Texas moved inside the Sooners' thirty-five. Simms threw a pass into the end zone, and for a moment it appeared that Texas's Sloan Thomas had caught it. But no, this was the OU defense, remember, and the person who wound up with the football was Perkins. That was one of four times that Simms would throw an interception that day, establishing a pattern of reversal that would drive Brown damn near out of Austin.

A signature Bob Stoops moment came with two minutes to play. Still leading 7–3, OU looked at fourth-and-two at the UT twenty-nine. Stoops deemed the long field a high-risk venture. Stoops's brother Mike, the defensive coach, offered a suggestion.

"I really think we ought to pooch kick and put the ball inside their ten," Mike said.

"All right. I'll go with that," said brother Bob.

The Sooners lined up as if to attempt the field goal, then had the holder pitch the ball to Tim Duncan, who attempted to feather the punt down near the Texas goal. He got too much of the ball, though, and it appeared headed for a sure touchback. Then UT safety (and future pro bowler) Nathan Vasher did an odd thing. He signaled for a fair catch at the Texas three-yard line. Vasher said afterward that from where he was standing, he thought the ball had been placekicked, and he wasn't sure what to do. "It didn't look like a regular field goal. Anything fishy, you have to go after."

Like Roy Williams would go after Chris Simms on the next play. The blitzing Williams slammed Simms as he threw a pass, the ball fluttering into Lehman's hands for an easy but very memorable Oklahoma touchdown. Bob Stoops's mastery of Mack Brown in the Big D mind-game was now in place, and it was something that the Sooners coach sustained for six years.

Epilogue

ore football players from the recent years of the Texas-Oklahoma series drive Chevy pickup trucks than any other brand.

Why? Because the last thing the players see as they descend into the fabled tunnel that leads to the Cotton Bowl playing surface is an artsy billboard touting the durable, all-purpose Chevy Silverado. Actually, the billboard is attached to the back of the big scoreboard that stands atop the seats in the south end zone, where players from both teams surge into the arena in a Category 6 emotional storm. The gridiron combatants see the billboard at eye level as they leave the locker room, and the visual display is so striking that the subliminal effect is irresistible.

Visualize the message: "You're heading into a nonstop, three-and-a-half-hour, bare-knuckle skull-buster, and if you ain't Chevy tough, them old boys on the other side of the field will rip your head off and shit down your neck."

I took the ceremonial tunnel run after wandering off from the North Texas Irish Festival at Dallas's Fair Park, an event at which conventional attire features full-figured men clad in camouflage kilts and scabbards containing bayonets. It was late winter, and the sky was a paler shade of blue than the October radiance that embraces the prairies at Texas-OU time.

Deep into the football off-season, the huge stadium stood empty, lonesome, forlorn. And *voilà*! The gate to the tunnel was open, as a work crew was involved with chores inside the arena. So I took the ceremonial walk down onto the field and stood at the south goal line, the exact spot where Steve Worster crashed over to win the 1966 game and where Quentin Griffin strolled over for his sixth touchdown of the game in 2000.

All of that and then some. It happened right here. This Cotton Bowl, cradle of a billion memories, is a site of more meaningful history than the Tower of London. In Dallas—a city of, for, and by the real estate developer—that's a death sentence. Dallas developers fear and abhor history even more than they do trees because they haven't devised strategies to exploit and cash in on either. The reality is that the people who pull the levers of finance in Dallas do have big plans for this hallowed home of gridiron greatness. Bulldoze it. Implode it. Put up the sign: PALACE TOP ESTATES — TOWN HOMES FROM $3 MILLION.

That day, surrounded by an ocean of empty seats, immersed in the near silence, I could not help but be swallowed by an overpowering sense of *gone*. The gloom factor was deepened by the distant wailing of the bagpipes from the Irish Festival. Nothing more morbid than those damn bagpipes. . . . I guess Danny Boy died again.

Gaze up at the upper tiers of the stadium and what one does not see is the circle of glassed-in luxury suite incubators, and any arena facility in the land cannot long endure without such amenities.

Since the Cotton Bowl has no full-time tenant, the city has been reluctant to invest in the modernization of a facility that is the location for two big games a year. After the 2010 game, the annual Dallas weekend of frenzy is positioned for a niche on the ever-lengthening list of things and events that are swept beneath the carpet of yesteryear.

Perhaps, after all, the time has come to end the Dallas version of this thing. The Texas Alcoholic Beverage Commission has taken to arresting people on charges of suspicion of being drunk in a bar. That was a bold stride initiated by the political leadership in Texas circa 2006, which is intent upon transforming the Lone Star mystique into a chickenshit police state. It's all rather unbelievable. A worldwide phenomenon such as Texas groping for a new identity. Such a place does not deserve a cultural celebration on the epic scale of a Texas-Oklahoma game.

So I turned and trudged back up and out of the Cotton Bowl tunnel. I am not going to suggest that the feeling was one you get after visiting your aging parents in a faraway city, and the gnawing sensation that this will be the last time you see them. Of course the notion of comparing a football stadium to a parent is absurd. But I can understand how so many people could—the fans of both teams who, as previously described in this narrative, are virtually married to the Texas-OU game.

It has been written that the game maintains a spiritual meaning to some fans. That's crap. There is nothing spiritual about a football game. This one, however, is personal as hell, and the Texas-OU weekend, for untold thousands of followers, serves as the focal point and anchor of events and relationships that have impacted these people for a lifetime.

Should Texas-OU go home-and-home (or even switch over to the House of Glitz, which will be the future home of a pro football team in Arlington), the impact and sense of loss will fall mostly upon the Oklahomans, whose fire and zeal provide the catalyst that make the annual Dallas collision so visceral, so genuine.

One of the most compelling utterances in the history of American courtrooms happened in the late 1970s in Oklahoma. A former high school football player was on trial for murder, and a key witness was Sam Pigeon, a Cherokee spiritualist who spoke only his native tongue. The highlight of his testimony came when an interpreter told the judge, "Your honor, there is no word for cheerleader in the Cherokee language."

Maybe not. I'll wager, however, that the Cherokees have a clearly translated term for "beat the hell out of TU."

Out here on the lost continent of God, guns, and goal-line stands, while the old mens' bodies fail them, the grudges remain deep and strong.

Acknowledgments

These should begin with the person who suggested the title of the book. That is Jim Donovan, a full-phase literary consultant who lives in the Dallas area. A long time ago Donovan played on a high school football team in Puerto Rico, and his coach was fond of telling his players, "You gotta run with the big dogs or piss with the puppies."

It was an unfortunate irony that the author, the very week that he began typing this manuscript, essentially wrecked his right hand in an accident that happened while he was running with a big dog. So additional gratitude goes to Dr. Arnold DiBella at the Baylor Medical Center, where Mickey Mantle and Tom Landry died, for his efforts to reconstruct the damage. You'd be amazed how much a person can miss his right hand when it's no longer available.

Certain information here was derived from two previously published books, primarily *Oklahoma vs. Texas: When Football Becomes War* by Robert Heard. Heard used to be a reporter for the Associated Press who was best known, perhaps, for being wounded by the tower assassin at the University of Texas when he was covering the massacre for the AP in 1966. Heard's AP colleagues remember him with deep measures of fondness. Heard used to travel around with big quantities of Coors beer, when it wasn't available in most parts of Texas, to cover assignments throughout the state and would sell it to the thirsty wire service newspeople.

I lifted a couple of dandy quotes from *The Bootlegger's Boy* by Barry Switzer, as told to Austin author Bud Shrake. While flipping through the pages of the book, I was astonished to find the exact line of lyrics from the song "Dear Oakie" that had already been written into this manuscript. That was entirely a coincidence, but let's face it, "Dear Oakie" is not exactly a mainstream American melody. I thought I was the only person in the world who'd ever heard the thing.

There are two passages in the manuscript that appear in italics. That means that I'm not the originator of the prose. In this case, John Steinbeck gets the credit, along with the man known only as Bill, whose heroic exploration of the drinking man's world offer riveting passages in the bestseller entitled *Alcoholics Anonymous* (pages 14 and 22 respectively).

I am especially obligated to the illustrious Texas artist Bob "Daddy-O" Wade for help that he rendered in this project, and more important, his wife, Lisa, because Daddy-O couldn't have done what he did without Lisa showing him how to do it.

Thanks to Carol Roark and Beth Andreesen at the Dallas Public Library, and to Sue Gooding at the State Fair of Texas. Also, I owe favors to Steve Conatser, Michael Hickey, Pat Culpepper, Brad Stribling, and Monk White.

Three Oklahomans—Clark Chambers, Joe Maxie, and Garvin Isaacs—provided considerable background material for *Big Dogs*. Chambers and Maxie exemplify the OU fight song. They're Sooner born, Sooner bred, and when they die they'll be Sooner dead. The same can't quite be said of Isaacs, since he went to TCU. But he's a native of Apache County, Oklahoma, and he articulates the OU fervor in very distinct terms.

The ultimate gratitude goes to my wife, Karen, who is to me what Harper Lee was to Truman Capote.

Index